10TH ANNIVERSARY EDITION

unprocessed

REVITALIZE YOUR HEALTH WITH WHOLE FOODS

10TH ANNIVERSARY EDITION

unprocessed

REVITALIZE YOUR HEALTH WITH WHOLE FOODS

CHEF AJ
WITH GLEN MERZER

Book Publishing Company
Summertown, Tennessee

For Charles and Bailey:
I love you even more than sweet potatoes.

MIX
Paper from responsible sources
FSC® C005010

Food photography: Hannah Kaminsky, hannahkaminsky.com
Chef AJ kitchen photography: Jamie Bergandi, jamiebergandiphoto.com
Chef AJ author photo: Gor Gevorkyan, royalgor.com
Chef AJ makeup: Sierra Bueno, officialbeautybybueno.com
Glen Merzer author photo: Robert Merrill, robertmerrillstudio.com
Stock photography: 123 RF
Cover and interior design: John Wincek, aerocraftart.com

Printed in the United States of America

BPC
PO Box 99
Summertown, TN 38483
888-260-8458
bookpubco.com

ISBN: 978-1-57067-408-2

27 26 25 24 23 22   3 4 5 6 7 8 9

> **Disclaimer:** The information in this book is presented for educational purposes only. It isn't intended to be a substitute for the medical advice of a physician, dietitian, or other health-care professional.

CONTENTS

E arth and its inhabitants are in big trouble: We are eating ourselves and our planet to death. Diet is the common denominator for mitigating the negative impacts of chronic diseases, climate change, and now viral pandemics. Each in its own right is threatening the lives of every human being on the planet. Progress in solving problems created by the first two challenges—chronic diseases and climate change—has been negligible; we seem content with eventual doom, barely noticing our demise, like the proverbial frog in the pot of water brought to a slow boil. Our ship is sinking, but yet not sunk.

The time has come for all hands to come on deck. People must take advantage of every reasonable solution to save ourselves. *Radical* would be to let destructive dietary behaviors continue, as they currently are, unchecked. Unfortunately, people are more reluctant to talk about their diets than they are about discussing religion and politics.

The truth is simple and easy to understand. Recall examples you have seen with your own eyes. Historical paintings and writings portray the obese king with his gout-inflicted foot propped on a stool, sitting among his sickly-looking royal court, before an opulent spread of animal foods (cows, pigs, chickens, and fishes), finished off with plate of pastries. Your eyes have witnessed how "rich" foods make people sick. Now is the time to speak out with whatever skills you may have, as a politician, a business leader, a public speaker, a writer, a singer, etc.

The wealthy class was once limited to only a few members. In contrast, the multitudes were hard-working people who obtained the bulk of their calories from beans, corn, potatoes, rice, and/or wheat, with a few in-season fruits and vegetables. These ordinary people were fit, trim, and healthy (as long as enough food was available). In the mid-1800s, with the Industrial Revolution and the harnessing of fossil fuels, wealth came to common folks, followed by a shift to foods once reserved for the privileged, and as expected, diseases of affluence quickly became epidemics, and now they are a pandemic (worldwide).

The story of healing common chronic diseases by making better choices at the dinner table has been told in many ways. One of the earliest descriptions of this "low-tech medicine" is provided by a controlled trial carried out nearly 2,600 years ago, and reported in the first chapter of Daniel of the Bible

(1:12-15): "*Daniel's men, who ate only starches and vegetables (pulses) and drank water for a study period of 10 days were found to be stronger, healthier, younger-looking, more-handsome, and/or without-blemish, when compared to men eating at the king's table.*" Based on these two undeniable observations, *diet-therapy* (the prevention and treatment of diseases by improvements in people's short- and long-term food patterns) should be the practice of medicine in the twenty-first century. It is not. My wife, Mary, and I have been working to fix this failing for a half century.

My professional rebellion against the standard practice of medicine began after medical school in the 1970s. I challenged my learned colleagues with scientific research demonstrating the superiority of diet-therapy over conventional treatments (most medications and non-emergency surgeries). Mary started the low-fat vegan revolution in 1983 with the publication of her recipes in our first national bestselling book, *The McDougall Plan.*

During our professional careers we have run two residential programs, developed two national food production companies and a travel business, and published thirteen national bestselling books (eleven with Mary). The McDougall Program is now internet-based, providing medical care, education, and ongoing support. Patients thrive under this modern mode of communication via computer screens.

Our treatment successes have been documented in three studies published in peer-reviewed scientific journals. Findings consistently show patients succeed in the short run, seven days, with an average weight loss of more than three pounds while fully satisfying their appetites, and in that time they experience a twenty-point reduction in cholesterol. Nearly 90 percent of patients reduced or stopped their medications, and most had hope for a cure. Long-term results showed 85 percent of people fully complied with the Program (the Diet) for at least a year, with an average weight loss of 20 to 25 pounds and a 20 mg/dl cholesterol reduction, as well as living medication-free and with hope for a healthier future. It took a half-century of hard work, but Mary and I did change the way people think about food preparation, nutrition, and medicine. In other words, we revived diet-therapy for patients all over the world. Now we are taking on a new patient: Planet Earth.

The same diet that allows individual patients to heal provides a real chance for saving our home. Al Gore's 2006 documentary, *An Inconvenient Truth*, first warned us of impending disasters from overheating the planet. The WorldWatch Institute (2009) concluded that livestock accounts for more than 51 percent of the greenhouse gases produced annually. The *EAT-Lancet Commission*, the most respected authority on diet and climate change, came to the conclusion (2020) that a worldwide change to a vegan diet would reduce greenhouse gas production by agriculture by as much as 80 percent.

The importance of a traditional diet, which prevents and cures most *comorbid* conditions, such as obesity, diabetes, and heart disease, has become apparent with the recent onset of viral pandemics (such as COVID-19). Comorbid conditions weaken our defenses enough to allow progression of a person harboring a contagion to hospitalization and to premature death. In other words, healthy people are usually asymptomatic or have only mild disease after infection.

In order to get Earth and its inhabitants out of big trouble, we are proposing a simple U-turn back to the traditional diets followed by nearly all humans.

All large populations of trim, healthy, athletic-competing, war-fighting people throughout verifiable human history have obtained the bulk of their calories from starches. Examples of thriving populations include the Japanese, Chinese, and other Asians, who ate sweet potatoes, buckwheat, and rice; and Incas in South America who ate potatoes. Mayans and Aztecs in Central America were known "as the people of the corn," and the Middle East, formally known as "the breadbasket of the world," fed hundreds of millions on a diet of wheat and barley. I use the past tense because since the early 1980s, animal food-rich eating patterns have prevailed over traditional diets worldwide. By no coincidence, over this same forty-year period, this change in food choices has brought our planet to the brink of extinction of all life on Earth.

Life on a dead planet sounds difficult, if not impossible. Let's take the easy way and fix the food now. Chef AJ is one of many soldiers battling for a food revolution that is long overdue.

February 19, 2011, is a day that I will never forget. I had the honor of giving a presentation at "The McDougall Advanced Study Weekend" in Santa Rosa, California. Afterwards, I had the opportunity to sell my very first book, *Unprocessed*. I sold over 100 copies that day and signed each one: "Eat Your Greens in Good Health!!! Love & Kale, Chef AJ." It was thrilling to become an author, and it marked the beginning of my path to becoming a passionate advocate of plant-based nutrition in a growing global movement.

Unprocessed is an imperfect book, but I did my best to tell my story and relay all the knowledge and information that I had at the time. When I wrote *Unprocessed*, I was fifty pounds overweight and had fluctuated between being overweight and obese my entire life.

Two weeks before *Unprocessed* was published, I was a patient at the True-North Health Center, where I learned about calorie density from Dr. Doug Lisle and Dr. Alan Goldhamer. But knowing and doing are two different things. A year later, I finally implemented all I had learned from them, and within a little over two years, I lost fifty pounds. With the help of my co-author, Glen Merzer, I went on to explain all that I had learned about calorie density and other approaches to healthy weight loss in our best-selling book, *The Secrets to Ultimate Weight Loss.*

Once I had slimmed down and improved my own health by eating a starch-based diet, as Dr. John McDougall has recommended for over forty years, I began to feel that many of the recipes in *Unprocessed* were too high in fat for some people to achieve their weight-loss goals. And I had made a mistake in putting the desserts at the front of the recipe section. But the key point of the book—to eat whole plant food, instead of animal products and processed food—I stand behind, and it remains central to my dietary philosophy today.

In the ten years since my personal health transformation, I've had the privilege of working with thousands of people and helping them to lose weight and manage their food addictions. In doing so, I employ all the strategies that we explain in depth in *The Secrets to Ultimate Weight Loss.* I mention that here because some of the healthy, whole-food ingredients that I use in the recipes of *Unprocessed,* such as dried fruit, nuts, seeds, nut butters, and seed butters like tahini, are simply too calorically dense for some people to eat on a regular basis and still be able to lose weight. And for those who suffer from food addictions, some of these foods may be trigger foods; in other words, once you start eating them, you have trouble stopping. If you're unable to moderate your use of a high-calorie food, and you don't cut it out of your diet completely, you're likely to struggle with your weight.

While I still contend that any refined oil is inflammatory and detrimental to your health, I do believe that whole-food fats, while calorically very dense, are not inherently unhealthy foods. But if you're struggling with your weight, you might want to greatly reduce your consumption of these foods—or simply omit them. The healthiest fats are the ones that are high in omega-3 fatty acids, which are also present in greens, but are particularly abundant in walnuts, flaxseeds, and chia seeds. My recommendation is to have a tablespoon or two of ground flax or chia seeds daily on your salad or oatmeal.

Although the dessert recipes in *Unprocessed* are higher in fat than most of the other recipes, I would argue that my bRAWnies, composed of dates, walnuts, and cocoa powder, are far healthier than a brownie made with sugar, flour, and oil.

So what has changed in this Tenth Anniversary Edition? First, we've added some beautiful color photographs by the enormously talented Hannah Kaminsky. We've also added more than thirty brand new, low-fat, healthy, and delicious recipes. As for the recipes from the original *Unprocessed,* with one exception (a recipe that contained alcohol that we've omitted) we still include every one as it appeared in 2011, but we also updated those that we could, by giving suggestions for lower fat options. For example, in some of the savory recipes, beans make a great substitute for the nuts, and in some of the dessert recipes, rolled oats can replace them. We also moved the dessert section to the end of the recipe section, where it belongs. I used to take the attitude, "Life is uncertain. Eat dessert first." Now I say, for a long, healthy life, eat veggies first.

I did not meet Dr. Alan Goldhamer until two weeks before *Unprocessed* was published, and it was only after gaining insights from him that I began to feel that another questionable aspect of the book involved the use of salt. While none of the recipes in the book used any type of table salt, some of them called for low-sodium miso and low-sodium tamari. I honestly thought that all the recipes in *Unprocessed* were SOS-free (free of sugar, oil, and salt), but I didn't realize that low-sodium miso and low-sodium tamari, though much lower in sodium than table salt, could still be considered salt. Tamari has 233 mg of sodium per teaspoon, an improvement over the 2,300 mg of sodium per teaspoon in salt. And an even lower sodium choice would be coconut aminos, a wheat-free and soy-free substitute for soy sauce that contains only 90 mg of sodium per teaspoon. It's possible to find low-sodium miso paste that contains as little as 110 mg of sodium per teaspoon. Quite a few well-known plant-based doctors, even including those who don't recommend salt, do allow miso and believe it's healthy.

Still, given my emphasis on SOS-free eating, it was a mistake to include recipes with low-sodium miso and low-sodium tamari while labeling them salt-free. Personally, I don't use these products anymore but would consider using them if I were preparing food for someone who was not used to eating a salt-free or low-sodium diet. There are so many more products on the market now that weren't available ten years ago that make SOS-free eating easy and enjoyable.

Just as *Unprocessed* was a good first book for me to write, I believe that it's a good first book for people transitioning to a plant-based diet. And many of the recipes are kid friendly. PCRM cooking instructor Sharon McRae bought the book at Vegetarian Summerfest in 2011 and was successfully able to transition her three children (a six-year-old and ten-year-old twins) to a plant-exclusive diet using recipes from *Unprocessed,* such as Easy Cheesy Peasies, bRAWnies, Sweet Potato Nachos, and Chef AJ's Disappearing Lasagna.

Since *Unprocessed* has been out for over ten years and we've heard from so many readers, we've had time to learn what the fan favorites are. We encourage you to try some of them: Chef AJ's Disappearing Lasagna, Perfect Pesto Stuffed Mushrooms, Hail to the Kale Salad, Quinoa Salad with Currants, Pistachios, and Pomegranate, and the Peanut Butter Fudge Truffles, to name but a few.

So while a few things have changed in this book, my fundamental beliefs about food have not. Processed food is not food. It may be readily available, easily affordable, and socially acceptable, but it's not meant for human consumption. Food is not meant to come from a can, a box, a bottle, or a bag. Like our ancestors, we are meant to eat our food from a plant, not manufactured in a plant.

I thank you for reading our book, and we wish you continued success on your journey to optimal health. Enjoy an Unprocessed life!

Love and Kale,
Chef AJ and Glen

My name is Abbie Jaye, but everyone calls me Chef AJ. I would like to briefly share with you my personal story and tell you what I have learned about nutrition from a life that has primarily revolved around food: (1) What we eat affects all aspects of our being, probably more than anything else we do. (2) What we eat has a profound effect on how we feel and look. (3) Food can cause disease, or it can prevent and reverse it. Unfortunately, I did not have this awareness until it was almost too late.

Like many people, I've experienced a great deal of suffering and loss in my life, but food was the one constant I could always count on. Sadly, food was the undoing of my parents, both of whom died from preventable, diet-related diseases (coronary artery disease and bowel obstruction), and food nearly destroyed my health as well. I battled food and my weight virtually every day of the first four decades of my life. Realizing this now not only makes me angry but also makes me even more determined to help others do better.

What we eat can be our undoing or our salvation. The distinction lies in the disparity between processed and unprocessed food. Actually, I'm being generous using the term "processed food," because the majority of these products barely qualify as being fit for consumption. When an item is basically nutrient-free, it's difficult to understand why we even consider it edible, especially when we know it doesn't nourish the body and only feeds the waistline.

Let me clarify what I mean by unprocessed versus processed food. The whole-food items found in the produce aisle or bulk section of a grocery store or supermarket are unprocessed; that is, they are more or less in the same state as when they were harvested. These include fruits, vegetables, legumes (beans, peas, and lentils), whole grains, nuts, and seeds. Packaged items that typically host a long list of ingredients fall into the processed category, which also includes foods that have been refined or concentrated. Sugar and oils top that list, along with the items they have been added to, such as Fruit Loops and potato chips. You get the idea.

When unprocessed (and only unprocessed) foods are combined, by cooking or blending, the outcome is, by my standards, unprocessed. My simple rule of thumb is this: If a dish can easily be made in your kitchen using whole ingredients, it's unprocessed. For example, you can cook lentils, carrots, onions, and spinach together to make a soup, so that's unprocessed. You can blend fresh or frozen fruits together to make a smoothie, so that's unprocessed. You can bake a potato or cook an ear of corn, as each of these is unprocessed. But you can't make vegetable oil or sugar or maple syrup or agave nectar. However, you can use whole dates as a sweetener, or you can use date syrup or date paste (see my recipe on page 146), both of which you can make in your kitchen, so they pass the test.

All the foods that pass my test contain fiber, which is satiating but contains very few calories. Foods that don't pass my test contain little or no fiber. The benefits of fiber to human health are gaining ever greater scientific appreciation.

Yes, there's a gray area between processed and unprocessed food. I don't often make applesauce in my kitchen, but if the only ingredient in a jar of applesauce is whole, ripe apples, it will pass my test. Tofu is another food I can't easily make in my kitchen, but it's a comparatively simple food made by boiling soybeans and adding nigari or calcium sulfate, coagulating agents that separate the curd, which is then pressed. Tofu has been made for thousands of years in Asia and is certainly a far less processed food than other meat alternatives that contain soy protein isolate, a highly refined product that has been used as a food ingredient only since 1959.

How about whole-grain bread: processed or unprocessed? Well, if the bread has sprouted organic whole wheat berries as its principal ingredient, it falls in the unprocessed side of the gray area. If the bread is made from white flour, it's in Fruit Loops territory, and, trust me, you don't want to go there. Here is how I would rank bread in general: sprouted whole-grain bread is better than bread made from whole wheat flour, and bread made from whole wheat flour is better than bread made from refined wheat flour or, worse yet, white flour. The superior choice is eating the whole grain itself from which the bread is made.

First and foremost, I'm an ethical vegan (Heck, I'm even in the Vegan Hall of Fame!) and am passionate about recommending a vegan diet—a diet containing zero animal products—to everyone. It's better for our health, better for the environment, and better for the animals. But purely from a health perspective, one could argue that we would be healthier eating a diet that is 90 percent vegan and 90 percent unprocessed than we would be eating a diet that is 100 percent vegan but 100 percent processed. It's very easy and convenient to eat a nutrient-deficient vegan diet, loaded with oil, sweeteners, fake meats, and refined grains. And while it's true that these foods don't require the death of an animal, they certainly won't help us achieve good health. Our biological protection comes from nutrient-rich whole foods, not from the good karma of grateful cows.

Now, let me tell you about my long and hard road to these dietary conclusions.

My Story

I was born in Chicago in 1960, shortly after the creation of isolated soy protein. That food substance was also created in the Windy City, which may explain my reaction to it. Both my mom and my grandmother were good cooks, and I began my culinary career at the age of seven, when I received an Easy-Bake Oven for Hanukkah. Oh how I loved watching that lightbulb magically turn batter into a real cake. I developed a serious sweet tooth early on, never realizing that my addiction to sugar could someday kill me.

In the early sixties, the processed food industry was just at the start of its ascendancy. Although we had a few processed food items, mainly in the form of sweetened breakfast cereals, we mostly ate *real food*. My mother, Lillian, cooked dinner for the family every night. Yes, we ate animal products, but there was always a salad and vegetable accompanying them, and if we wanted dessert, we had to clean our plates first. I'm not saying this is the best way to raise kids, but at least I did eat vegetables and I liked them. I didn't grow up like the kids you see on *Jamie Oliver's Food Revolution,* who can't even identify broccoli. I always loved broccoli; unfortunately, I loved all things sweet even more.

I was overweight growing up and became obese by age eleven. I weighed 160 pounds and was not yet five feet tall. (What's interesting is that if I could magically transport today's youths back to my childhood, I would fit right in with them by today's standards.) I got teased a lot, so I compensated by being a straight-A student. But to a teenager, academic satisfaction pales in comparison to not being asked to your senior prom because you're too fat. Being fat hurts, inside and out.

I suffered my first major bout of depression in my early teens, when I was abandoned by my father, who was physically and emotionally abusive. Psychologists say that early childhood trauma like this can affect brain chemistry in such a way that makes it even harder for a person to deal with future adversities. When my father abandoned my family, I was sent to live in California with an aunt and uncle and two cousins. Almost two years passed before I was reunited with my mother, and although I was deeply depressed over our separation, in hindsight, it was the best thing that could have happened to me for a variety of reasons. Besides being transported to a new, loving family, I now had my aunt's mother, Memé, living with us. Memé was a graduate of Le Cordon Bleu and did all the cooking in the home. When I think about what I eat today and how I teach my classes, I realize that the seeds of my success were planted early on by this wonderful Swiss lady. This was a woman who not only cooked real food but also made it gourmet. She could make anything taste delicious. During the time I lived with her, my favorite food was *leeks!*

Watching Memé prepare meals was better than anything you could see on the Food Network today. Every meal was like eating at a five-star restaurant. She would go to the store and buy whatever was fresh and in season and create a culinary masterpiece. And she never used recipes or measured anything! (This is how I prepare food today, and that's why it's taken me so long to write a cookbook.) Because my aunt and her mother were European, we had salad after the meal, and we always had lots of fruits and veggies too. Even Memé's desserts were primarily whole foods, like her pear galette. Although she did use sugar, flour, and butter, her pastries were not overly sweet, oily, or salty, in contrast to what passes for dessert today. The entire time I lived with the Harter family was a gastronomic delight. My taste buds were spoiled, and I became somewhat of a snob. When my mom finally was able to come out to California, I turned up my nose one evening when she served, of all things, Cool Whip!

Leaving the Harter family home (and all that great food) was yet another loss and yet another adjustment. I went from a loving home where there were people around all the time to a tiny apartment with just my mom, who now had to work full time. And so began my digestive decline. My mom was an excellent cook, but she no longer had time to lovingly prepare our meals from scratch the way she did when she was a homemaker in Chicago. So I do understand the plight of today's working parents. More often than not, dinner was something my mom picked up on her way home, such as Kentucky Fried Chicken (extra crispy, of course). Gone were the days of a vegetable at every meal and salad for dessert. We were on our way to becoming junk food junkies.

I tried to make real food, but when you're thirteen without a car or an allowance, it ain't easy. I did try to cook some of our meals and occasionally surprised my mom with steamed vegetables and brown rice for dinner. I gave my first formal dinner party at the age of fourteen; I even sent out actual invitations. Using the Time-Life cookbooks, I made Cornish game hens with apple chestnut stuffing, braised hearts of celery, and, for dessert, a bourbon caramel custard cream pie.

I was on my way to becoming a great chef . . . until high school happened. Because I skipped the fourth grade, I was always younger than everyone else in my class. I was also significantly heavier, now that I had slipped over to the dark side (eating processed food). Once, a hurtful comment about my weight led me to stop eating for seven days straight. That was my first bout with anorexia nervosa, and my dreams of becoming a chef would be crushed for another twenty-five years. I wound up battling this serious eating disorder for the next eleven years.

As a junior at the University of Pennsylvania, my anorexia became so severe and my weight so low that I had to be hospitalized for several months. I was scared to be all alone in a hospital in Philadelphia, so I was transferred to one in Los Angeles. I still remember the embarrassment and shame I felt when my sister-in-law, Lauren, picked me up to take me home.

There weren't any state-of-the-art treatments for anorexia in the late seventies, so the "treatment" protocol went more or less like this: "Either you eat or we stick a tube down your throat and feed you." I had the choice of either eating crappy hospital food or being tubed. I chose the former. (Did you ever wonder why people who could benefit from good nutrition the most, like hospital patients and schoolchildren, are served the worst-quality food?) Oh, and they had someone watching us at all times, so we couldn't purge and they wouldn't let us exercise. I ate what they served so I could put the weight back on and get the hell out of there. The nurse told me how I had permanently damaged myself with this disease and how I had really screwed up my hypothalamus and liver and other organs. I didn't care; I just wanted to go home, and I was willing to do anything to get out of the hospital.

While I was hospitalized for anorexia, I developed some serious medical complications. Unlike many Americans who worry unnecessarily about this condition, I actually was protein deficient. But, as any plant-based doctor will tell you, you can't be protein deficient without being calorie deficient, and I was literally starving myself to death. My hair and fingernails fell out, and I stopped getting menstrual periods. An endoscopy showed that the vomiting I did after bingeing had burned my esophagus. I was very sick, but I was also very difficult to deal with. I will always regret what I put my family through.

Unfortunately, when I did start eating again, I didn't choose a plant-based, nutrient-rich, whole-food diet. I chose crap. All the treats I had been denying myself for years I now devoured with abandon. That kicked my sugar addiction into full gear. I was on a first-name basis with every salesperson at Weby's and Skandia bakeries, and I knew what was inside every piece of See's Candy just by looking at it from the outside. My nightly dinner became a hot fudge sundae from Baskin-Robbins with Baseball Nut or Pralines 'n Cream ice cream. Double fudge, extra nuts.

That was bad enough, but on top of it, I also completely stopped eating fruits and vegetables. I was required to gain only twenty pounds to no longer be underweight and get out of the hospital, but I literally could not stop eating hyper-palatable food composed of the perfect combination of sugar, fat, and salt. My new way of eating really put the anorexia behind me: I ended up gaining sixty pounds! That was thirty pounds more than I weighed before I started losing weight on my journey to anorexia.

So now, for the first time in my adult life, I was officially obese. Due to my messed-up GI system, I could no longer force myself to vomit, so in order to lose weight, I began to exercise . . . and I became addicted to that too. I also intentionally took up smoking cigarettes, a habit I always abhorred, because I thought it would help me lose weight. (Thankfully, I was forced to quit just a few years later due to a broken rib.) Anyway, addiction is addiction is addiction. Those of us whose brain chemistry allows us to quickly and easily become addicted to one substance also can easily become addicted to another. I never realized I had an addiction problem because my doctor had said that sugar is not addictive! But, of course, it is, and that's why food manufacturers (a fitting name, "food manufacturers") put it in everything from infant formula to geriatric formula.

Within months of getting out of the hospital, I had become extremely ill. I had developed adult-onset asthma and needed to take hundreds of dollars' worth of medication every month. I was constantly injecting myself with epinephrine. Then I was in a serious accident in which my spine was crushed. I was temporarily paralyzed and in a body cast for a year. The "upside" of that experience? You can't binge while you're in a body cast, as it's too tight. These myriad illnesses and injuries ended up depleting all the benefits on my mom's health insurance, and I was dropped. Needless to say, I had hit rock bottom.

Unable to continue on like this, I turned to God. Maybe not the most original move for an addict, but it worked for me. I didn't join a twelve-step program (is there even a Sweet Tooth Anonymous?); I began a spiritual practice that involved yoga and meditation. I also read a book that made a lasting impression on me: *You Can Heal Your Life* by Louise Hay. Probably for the first time ever, I hit my knees and prayed to God. I remember saying, "Please just allow me to eat like a normal person and I will accept any weight you want me to be as long as I can easily maintain it without fasting, bingeing, or overexercising." In retrospect, since it appears that someone was listening, the wording of my prayer may have been a strategic mistake. I should have asked to be thinner.

My late twenties and thirties were somewhat happier times, as I began acting and performing comedy. I realized a lifelong dream by appearing on several television shows, including *The Tonight Show Starring Johnny Carson,* where I performed my signature act of playing two flutes through my nose while standing on my head and blowing bubble gum out of my mouth. I also met my husband, Charles. We got married in 1995, the same year I graduated college.

We took a Mexican cruise on our honeymoon, and being the accident-prone Aries that I am, something told me to buy the insurance. Boy, am I glad I did. I developed a life-threatening lung and liver infection in Ensenada, and my hospital bill for just three days was over twenty thousand dollars. I learned again, as if I ever needed reminding, that the only thing I hate more than going to a funeral is being a patient in a hospital.

After I got married, I started having some knee pain from doing step aerobics, so I had to take a break from it. During the resultant inactivity, I gained some weight. This was the time when the drug fen-phen, the so-called miracle weight-loss drug, was at its height of popularity. My doctor prescribed it for me, and I lost tons of weight easily and effortlessly, and I felt great mentally too. In fact, I had never felt better! Although I was still eating crap, with the addition of fen-phen my brain was tricked into eating less of it. Then the FDA pulled the drug off the market due to serious heart and lung side effects. I had an echocardiogram to see if I had sustained any valve damage, and luckily, I hadn't.

But it wouldn't be long before my horrible diet would catch up with me.

When I was thirty-nine, I finally got pregnant. Charles and I had tried for so many years, and we were both so excited. In January 2000, though, I began bleeding, and my OB/GYN wanted to do an amniocentesis. I knew there were risks involved with this procedure, so I initially declined. But the doctor said it was vital to know what was going on with the baby prior to delivery, and he convinced me to have it.

A funny thing happened during that procedure—my husband (not me) fainted. Many years would pass before I would find anything funny again. The results came back that the baby, a girl whom we had named Rachel and who had waved to us during the last ultrasound, had Down's syndrome. I was devastated, but I still wanted to have the baby. The doctor said there was more we needed to know and recommended that we immediately see a high-risk neonatologist because in three days the state of California would deem the baby a live birth, and I would not be able to do anything about it.

Seeing the high-risk neonatologist was one of the worst days of my life. The doctor said that the baby had no tricuspid valve and had a hole in each of the four chambers of her heart. If she did make it to term, she would need to have immediate and frequent open-heart surgeries. We had twenty-four hours to decide whether we wanted to terminate the pregnancy. Charles and I decided we did not want her to suffer, so I signed the consent form allowing the doctor to terminate the "flawed pregnancy."

I wouldn't wish the loss of a child on my worst enemy. What made it worse was when people would say things like, "Well, it wasn't a real baby." Let me tell you, the minute you find out you're pregnant, *it is real* and you are already in love with this person you've never even met. I fell into another deep depression. I didn't even want to live anymore. But I didn't have time to grieve for long. I received a call from an ICU nurse in Illinois who told me that my father was very ill.

Even though I had seen my father only twice from the age of eleven to the age of forty, he had made me the executor of his will. The laws are different in Illinois, so I had to fly back there, still bleeding from my own operation, to manage the end of his life. He had suffered from coronary artery disease even before I was born. He had his first heart attack before the age of fifty. Although he wasn't overweight like my mother, he did have high blood pressure and high cholesterol and ate the standard American diet, with a Jewish twist. He loved his daily slice of kosher salami like a bunny loves carrots. In the end, it killed him. He was already on all the medications you can be on for heart disease and nothing had helped. He had overcome prostate cancer but couldn't tolerate the daily chest pains. So he opted for open-heart surgery, which failed. I watched him languish in the ICU the last nineteen long days of his life, as he was first put on a ventilator, then a feeding tube, then a tracheotomy tube. His hands were tied down so he would not pull the tubes out. He could not speak, but you could see the terror in his eyes as he wasted away for almost three weeks in a helpless state. And for what? For his love of kosher salami.

Kosher salami, for anyone who is taking notes, differs from regular salami in that one kills you and the other is blessed by a rabbi before it kills you.

After I lost my baby and then my dad, my beloved dog, Scooby, died. Then my mom developed severe dementia and congestive heart failure, all caused by her diet. I became her primary caregiver during the last four years of her life and watched her deteriorate slowly and insidiously.

During that terrible time in my life, I suffered three more miscarriages and required multiple operations to correct problems caused by a piece of fetal thoracic bone that lodged in my uterus from the death of the first baby. When I left my home, I began having panic attacks, but I couldn't take medication for them during the periods when I was pregnant.

After my last operation, the surgeon said that he was sorry, but I would not be able to have children. Like a computer that crashes, my brain completely short-circuited. I couldn't work, so I quit my job, and we wound up losing our home. I developed panic disorder with agoraphobia so severe that until Sparky was trained to be my service dog, I didn't leave my house for almost a year.

All the emotional trauma I suffered took a toll on my diet and my health. My sugar addiction went through the roof. I was so depressed that I didn't want to eat, and if I did, it had to be something sweet. They say "to grieve well is to live well," and I was doing a pretty poor job at both. One of the teachers at Dick and Jane Cook Vegetarian, the culinary school where I was teaching, told me that I was eating all this sugar to compensate for the lack of sweetness in my life. I had a few choice words to say to him, but I sure wish I could find him now so I could apologize and tell him he was right.

For years, this is what my diet consisted of: Breakfast was a thirty-two ounce Coke Slurpee with eight pumps of vanilla syrup, and lunch was a forty-eight ounce Big Gulp Dr. Pepper. During this time, I was working sixty hours a week as an activity director at a retirement home. By 4:00 p.m., I couldn't keep my eyes open, so I would have some type of vegan pastry. Thankfully, Javier, the chef at the facility, would make steamed broccoli with marinara sauce for me every night before I went home. It was my only real sustenance. I would leave my job exhausted and feeling really down about myself, knowing that practically nothing I ate that day remotely resembled food. Ultimately, I got an inescapable wake-up call.

During the morning of January 1, 2003, I tried to have a bowel movement. Instead, the entire toilet bowl was filled with bright-red blood. I was terrified. My grandmother had died of colon cancer, my mom and my other grandmother had died of a bowel obstruction, and one of my uncles had recently had 80 percent of his colon removed. I was worried that something was seriously wrong. I contacted my HMO and said that I wanted a colonoscopy, but my request was denied. The representative stated that only having a first-degree relative with cancer would warrant the procedure for me and that I probably just had hemorrhoids. Hemorrhoids? I had had a hemorrhoidectomy in 1985, and, at their worst, my hemorrhoids never bled profusely like this. After jumping through all the HMO's crazy hoops, I finally received a sigmoidoscopy, which, sure enough, showed that I had several large, bleeding adenomatous polyps in my sigmoid colon. These are the kind that, if not removed, usually become malignant. The doctors called them "precancerous," and that was a big enough wake-up call for me. My colon was so filthy and in such bad shape from forty-three years of abuse that the doctors said they could not remove the polyps because they couldn't get "a clean shot." Even though I did the awful prep that's required before a procedure, they were only able to photograph the polyps but not remove them without risking serious infection. They told me I would have to come back for further intervention. Well, if there is one benefit of my panic disorder, it's that I am deathly afraid of taking most medications and having most procedures. Above all, I have an extreme fear of surgery and general anesthesia. When I had an endoscopy, I was so afraid of even the "light sedation" that they performed the whole procedure while I was completely awake.

So, instead of drugs or surgery, I took a different path that would forever alter the course of my life. I used diet. I figured that if my poor food choices could cause or at least greatly contribute to this disease, wouldn't it also be possible for better food choices to reverse it? Consequently, I opted to go the "drastic route"—as healthy dietary changes are often called—and on Sunday, July 6, 2003, I had my last Coke Slurpee and checked into the Optimum Health Institute (OHI) in San Diego, California. While it may be true that I have a genetic predisposition for developing colon cancer, genetics only account for 1 to 3 percent of cancer diagnoses. Genetics may load the gun, but diet and lifestyle pull the trigger!

Going to OHI would prove to be one of the best decisions I've ever made. There I met interesting people from all over the world, including celebrities who were there to lose weight and pro football players who were there to make weight before the season started. But there were also many guests who had very serious illnesses, such as brain cancer, lupus, and even AIDS. OHI is not a medical facility, and we were not allowed to even talk about our diseases or, as the staff called them, our "health opportunities." But every Friday, graduates of the program would come back and give testimonials of their healing, and I was deeply moved. They had diseases far more serious than mine, so I figured getting rid of these polyps would be a piece of cake, or should I say kale?

Every day, from morning until night, I took classes that dealt with healing on three levels: body, mind, and spirit. But the most important education I got was at mealtime. The diet OHI prescribed was not only plant based but also organic and 100 percent raw. And, unlike the diet of many raw foodists today that includes tons of highly processed, low-nutrient foods (such as agave nectar, coconut oil, and olive oil), the OHI diet was free of what I have come to call "The Evil Trinity" (sugar, oil, and salt). Instead, it was based on fruits, vegetables, sprouts, and seeds. For breakfast, we had watermelon. For lunch, a salad with vegetables, sprouts, and seed cheese made from sesame and sunflower seeds. Dinner was the same. Notably, there was no dressing and no dessert!

On three days of the seven-day program we did a juice fast; I thought I was gonna die. I would call my husband and sister every night and beg them to get me out of there. Like every addict who eventually comes clean, I was going through severe withdrawal and detox. Every day, in addition to the food we ate, we drank something called rejuvelac, plenty of water, and juice made from freshly grown wheatgrass. Colonics were optional, but we were instructed on how to give ourselves daily enemas and wheatgrass implants. For a woman who had stood on her head on *The Tonight Show,* this wasn't hard.

I have always had a "when in Rome" attitude, so I complied with the program 100 percent. At OHI, the abiding philosophy is that disease occurs when the body is in an acidic state, and that pretty much everything consumed on the standard American diet (meat, cheese, dairy, eggs, sugar, flour, caffeine, alcohol, oil, salt, processed food) serves to make the body acidic. We were taught that we need to alkalize our bodies, not by drinking some expensive water but by eating raw fruits and vegetables.

Abstaining from animal products wasn't a problem for me, but I had spent four decades eating from my own set of the four basic food groups: sugar, flour, oil, and caffeine. I remembered that at my fortieth birthday party at the Excalibur Hotel in Las Vegas, my family had roasted me. Charles had said, "My wife is the only vegetarian who never eats fruits or vegetables. The only greens she gets are in a bag of Skittles." He was right.

Today, while I empathize with my students who tell me it's hard for them to give up animal products, initially it was just as hard for me to go from my vegan junk-food diet to the diet I enjoy and advocate today.

When I got back from OHI, I felt better physically and emotionally than I had my entire life. I was slimmer and looked healthier and younger. My skin was clear and my eyes sparkled. When I arrived home, I was so calm and serene that my own dogs didn't recognize me. They looked confused and kept sniffing me as if they didn't know who I was. At home, I continued with the diet and the visualization techniques I had learned at OHI. For everyone it's different, but because my husband loves the game Pac-Man, every day I would visualize the little yellow man going through my colon and eating up the polyps as the video game theme song played in my head.

Six months later, I went for a follow-up sigmoidoscopy, and my colon was completely clear! The doctors said it was remarkably clean this time, pink and vascular like a newborn's, and they kept poking and prodding me, looking for the polyps to remove. They said they had photographs indicating their size and exact location, and now they were completely gone. They even accused me of going outside the HMO to get them removed! I told them that all I did was change my diet, and they said, "That's impossible!" Afterward, one of the doctors, who happened to be from India, quietly whispered in my ear, "I believe you."

Well, I believed me too. I knew that a series of emotional traumas, one after the other, had aggravated my tendency to turn to sweet, fatty, and salty foods for comfort, and that sweets in particular had become an addiction. I knew that my addiction had eventually threatened my health and my life. And I knew that eating whole, raw, unprocessed food had done what my doctors believed was impossible: restore my health and save me from their interventions.

I was elated by this news, but I knew that if I was going to keep eating this way, it would have to include more than sprouts and wheatgrass. It would have to taste delicious! So I took a leave of absence from my job and went to culinary school. Even though it was a raw vegan culinary school (Living Light Culinary Institute), the food was much richer than the food they taught us to eat at OHI. Every recipe had salt and either coconut oil or olive oil. They also used agave nectar, which had just been introduced as a "healthy" sweetener.

Nevertheless, I was consuming a massive quantity of fruits and veggies on a daily basis, so I was still way ahead nutritionally compared to where I had previously been. I started my days with a green smoothie made with one-half pound of spinach or kale. (I now eat a full pound of cooked greens for breakfast instead.)

Two years after my polyp diagnosis, I finally enrolled with a PPO. I immediately went back to my regular doctor and told him about my situation. He did a colonoscopy, reported that all was clear, and said that I didn't have to come back for another ten years.

After two years on a raw vegan diet, I started to eat cooked vegan food again, while making sure I also ate plenty of raw fruits and vegetables. I had researched whole-food diets and concluded that although following a strict raw-food regimen was invaluable for reversing my disease, it's possible to stay healthy and thrive while also including some cooked whole foods. The most important lesson I had learned at OHI was to eliminate white sugar and white flour without exception, as well as almost all processed food. I've never wavered from that directive, and I've never regretted it.

My dietary objective became, quite simply, to eat a whole-food, plant-based diet with no added sugar, oil, or salt and absolutely no processed food.

More than twenty years earlier, I had learned about not using oil when I read The McDougall Plan by John McDougall, MD. Dr. McDougall often says, "The fat you eat is the fat you wear." Even though I knew that oil was calorie dense and unhealthy, it wasn't until I read Prevent and Reverse Heart Disease by Caldwell B. Esselstyn, Jr., MD, that I learned how much it contributes to cardiovascular disease, which my father had died from. Dr. Esselstyn talks about the brachial artery tourniquet test and how even a single meal with oil can injure the endothelial lining of the arteries. I realized that oil (I'm looking at you, extra-virgin olive oil) is not only *not* a heart-healthy food but it's also injurious to the body and helps promote diabetes and heart disease.

Clearly, the oil had to go. What was fascinating is that when we gave up oil, my husband, who was never overweight, lost twenty-five pounds without making any other dietary changes. Seven months after we had cut oil out of our diet, an unsightly tumor on his spine shrank to the size of a nickel! I can only wonder what eliminating oil would do for cancer.

Salt was really not at all difficult for me to give up. Sure, I would put salt in a recipe that called for it, but I never added it to my food. My grandparents and parents already had advanced heart disease by the time I was born, so I grew up not eating salt. I remember that when I was seven years old someone gave me a pretzel rod with coarse salt on the outside. I took one bite and nearly puked. It tasted like an ocean wave had hit me and I swallowed all that salt water. If you grow up without eating salt, you really don't crave it.

There are many culinary tricks I will teach you later on that will help you curb your salt tooth, but in the meantime, if you still *must* consume it, do as Dr. McDougall advises and only sprinkle it on the surface of your food (what we chefs call "the finish"). Never cook with salt, as you will end up using way too much and the flavor will dissipate. One teaspoon of salt contains 2,300 milligrams of sodium. If you feel compelled to add salt to your food, coconut aminos, which have 90 milligrams of sodium per teaspoon, would be a better choice; a low-sodium miso would also be a healthier option.

But what about sugar? I had completely given up white sugar on July 6, 2003, and was now consuming only agave and maple syrup. Yet I now learned that they both are nutritionally indistinguishable from white sugar. As with oil, the only amount of sugar that's safe to eat is none. Although maple syrup and molasses may contain trace amounts of minerals, no one consumes processed sweeteners to satisfy their minimum daily requirement for minerals. Likewise, no one sprinkles processed sweeteners on their broccoli. Sugars and syrups are used to sweeten foods that are already unhealthy and nutritionally bereft, products that are primarily composed of flour and oil. If you ask me today what the healthiest sweetener is, I will tell you none. And if you ask me what the healthiest dessert is, I will tell you fruit.

I remember Dr. T. Colin Campbell joking about these three ingredients: "Sugar, oil, flour—that's a doughnut!" But I had been working as a pastry chef, and these were the three ingredients I was using the most! I thought I was doing customers a favor by using agave and maple syrup instead of sugar, by using spelt or barley flour instead of white flour, and by using coconut oil instead of butter. Desserts were my life, both making them and eating them. How could it be that the three main ingredients in desserts are actually the worst things (not counting animal products) for anyone to consume? I had never thought about how processing a food could make it more calorie rich and nutrient poor.

I was trying to support a friend who had a cancer diagnosis by joining him on a three-week, whole foods, plant-exclusive diet without any sugar, oil, or salt. The sugar-free part, though, was tripping me up. The seeker in me really wanted to figure out why I could not go one day, let alone three weeks, without a sweet treat. Whenever I would open the freezer, I would start bawling. It wasn't the kind of crying that happens with a stubbed toe. It was like the wailing of a frightened little kid in a department store who can't find his mommy. I was crying from the depths of my soul. I was crying inconsolably, the same way I did when Rachel had passed away. It had been almost eight years since she had died, and I realized I had never fully grieved for her or let go of the pain from our decision to terminate the pregnancy. It was so much easier to medicate myself with food, my drug of choice being dessert. I could get through the day without my "drug" by keeping constantly busy, always in motion. Once I was home, in the quiet of the night, I simply could not stand being alone with my thoughts and feelings. It was so much easier to eat a few homemade vegan chocolate-cherry cookies with crystallized ginger and just numb out. I kept telling myself, "It's only grief. It's not going to kill me," and "This too shall pass." And it did.

The three weeks passed and, after being off processed sugar, my palate readjusted. Now, for the first time in my life, I could taste the sweetness of fruit, and I loved it. A frozen grape tasted like sorbet from a fine restaurant. I fell in love with Gala apples, pluots, and Mexican papaya. Sometimes when I eat fruit now it tastes almost too sweet to me. Whether it's sugar or salt, your palate will readjust and you will start appreciating the sweetness and saltiness inherent in all whole plant foods. But this won't happen if you constantly stimulate your taste buds with sugar and salt. Remember, the *only* thing that cures addiction is complete and total abstinence. Moderation does not help an addict.

How Bad Do You Want It?

I hope that my life's story has piqued your interest about the many benefits of eating a whole-food plant-based diet, free of sugar, oil, and salt. Perhaps you're already convinced that this is the best way to eat but still believe that you could never do it.

Well, you should know by now that I didn't start eating this way overnight. It took almost fifty years to find the diet that worked best for me, so I don't expect you to do it all at once either. Unless you currently have a serious illness, such as cancer, heart disease, or diabetes, I wouldn't encourage you to dive in all at once, unless you are an "all or nothing" personality type and are certain you can handle it. My best advice is to just do *something*. Simply because you can't do everything doesn't mean you shouldn't do anything. Optimum health exists on a continuum and even small, incremental changes made consistently over time can still be of great benefit. For instance, take my student Matthew. He was not ready to do everything all at once. But he agreed to replace his standard American breakfast with a green smoothie every day, and within a year, he lost thirty pounds and went to his forty-fifth high school reunion at his senior class weight. Only you can decide what your personal health goals are and how quickly you want to attain them.

Like many people, you may have been eating a poor diet for a very long time. The longer you have been eating this way, the harder it may be for you to overhaul your diet and the more difficult your period of detox and withdrawal may be. But by no means is that a reason to avoid making a change. The first step in any journey is making a conscious decision to embark on it. Despite all the convincing evidence about how to lose weight and how quick and easy it can be to reverse the symptoms of common diseases caused by diet and lifestyle, maybe you just aren't ready. I have often found that the sicker people are, the more willing they are to make major changes immediately. If you aren't ready now, that's okay. If you want to wait until your health deteriorates further, that's always an option. Just keep this book on hand for when you become sick enough or fat enough that making a change is no longer avoidable. Or give it to someone else whose life may be saved by this information.

If you truly think you are prepared to start your journey toward optimal health and your ideal weight, the first step is to make a commitment that you will follow this plan for at least thirty days. You really only have two choices in life: You can either commit to doing something or you can pledge allegiance to your excuses for why you can't do it. If you're a *Star Wars* fan, you know what Yoda would tell you: "Do . . . or do not. There is no try." If you follow this program as prescribed for thirty days and do not see an improvement in your health, let me know, because you'll be the first. While you are following the program, aim for progress, not perfection. Do you know anyone who eats perfectly all the time? I do not. I am not perfect, and I am not asking you to be perfect. All I am asking from you is a serious commitment to a new approach to eating for a period of thirty days. If you continue, you may find that your diet will become healthier over time, just as mine did, in the ten years since *Unprocessed* was first published. Do you think you're up for the challenge?

I can hear the little voice in your head screaming, "Yeah, but . . ." If you are what I lovingly call a YABBUT, let's go over some of the common false beliefs people have when embracing a new, healthier lifestyle. I call them myths because I am able to debunk each of them. If you really want to do something, you'll find a way; if you don't, you'll find an excuse. The fact that you are even reading this book tells me that you are the kind of person who can see the possibility of something wonderful for your life, for your health, and for the health of your family. I'm guessing you've already successfully overcome many challenges in your life, so why should this be any different?

I studied acting with a brilliant teacher named Joan Darling. She won an Emmy for directing a hilarious episode of *The Mary Tyler Moore Show* called "Chuckles Bites the Dust." My acting class had a vast mix of participants, ranging from a young child who had never acted to Academy Award–nominated actors. Many would ask Joan if they had what it took to succeed as a professional actor, using the phrase, "Have I got it?" Joan's answer was always the same: "How bad do you want it?" I am giving you all the tools you need to succeed and to have boundless energy and amazing health. You only have to ask yourself one question and answer it honestly: How bad do you want it?

YABBUT #1: It's too expensive to eat this way.

It is absolutely true that fast food and processed foods are cheap, quick, and easy. But if you continue to eat them, please also know that recovering from heart bypass surgery or foot amputation from diabetes is expensive, slow, and difficult. It's interesting how many people come to my classes and say they can't afford to eat this way, while they are carrying the largest designer coffee from Starbucks (and you know this wasn't their first visit there). They are paying at least five dollars a day for their favorite drugs: caffeine and sugar. Many of them are also wearing Lululemon leggings. It really is a matter of priorities. If your health was a priority, we wouldn't even be having this conversation. You're an adult and you have every right to choose to eat whatever you want. (But, by the way, I don't believe you should have the right to feed that same crap to your children.)

Although it's accurate to say that it can be more expensive to eat an unprocessed diet, especially at the start, it doesn't have to be. There are free online resources that show how this way of eating can actually be less expensive than a junk-food diet (see drmcdougall.com and forksoverknives.com).

Many people say they can't afford organic food. Of course, I certainly want to support organic farming practices whenever possible, but, as Matthew Lederman, MD, says: "People are not fat and sick because they choose to eat conventionally grown produce instead of organic. They're fat and sick because they are not eating fruits and vegetables." I have seen huge bunches of organic kale on sale for ninety-nine cents a bunch. When you see great prices like that, stock up. Can't afford ninety-nine cents? Even discount stores, such as Walmart and 99 Cents Only Stores, stock many organic foods now. You can also buy frozen fruits and veggies, which are often more nutritious than their fresh counterparts. That's because fresh produce often sits on a truck for a week after it's been harvested before it gets to stores. Frozen fruits and vegetables are harvested when they're at their peak and then flash frozen, so very few nutrients are lost. These items are often on sale at local grocery stores, so stock up. Just be sure that the fruit you buy has no sugar added. Almost every city has a farmers' market now, and that's a great place to buy fresh, affordable produce. In addition, it's easy and economical to grow your own sprouts.

A large part of your diet should be composed of starchy vegetables, whole grains, and legumes. These items aren't costly to begin with, but if you buy them in the bulk section of the store, they are priced even lower. Potatoes, beans, and rice are some of the least-expensive foods you can buy.

You know how when you really want something in life, you somehow find the money for it? Well, if you really want your food to cost as little as possible, grow it yourself. But if you still aren't ready to eat this way, that's okay. It just means more kale for me!

YABBUT #2: I don't have the time to prepare healthy food.

This one really cracks me up because many people couldn't even sit through one of my classes without constantly checking their phone. You can see the angst in their eyes when their beloved handheld device makes a sound and I ask them to turn it off; they react as though they would die. I can't tell you how many times

I've gone on Facebook or Instagram after one of my classes and read posts students made during the class. Just as you can't safely drive while texting, you can't learn what I have to teach you if you are tethered to your phone during my class. For many people, technology is an addiction (just like white cupcakes with buttercream frosting and rainbow sprinkles used to be for me). When you're constantly connected electronically, you don't ever have to be alone, but your "time-saving" device somehow manages to leave you with no time for anything else. How much time do you spend on Facebook or Twitter or blogging, texting, and checking your email? How much time do you spend surfing the web, playing video games, or watching TV? The truth is, we all have enough time for the things we value. If your health and the health of your family truly are your top priority, time will cease to be an issue.

Eating the whole plant foods your body was designed to consume will give you so much energy that you will get things done more quickly and will end up having *more time*. In the recipe section of this book, you will learn ways to prepare wholesome food that take less time from start to finish than the preparation alone takes for conventional cooking. Let's consider soup preparation, for example. A standard soup recipe almost always begins with sautéing an onion in several tablespoons of oil. Well, that step takes time. For my soup recipes, all the ingredients are thrown in at once, often without any prep at all! And don't be concerned about how my recipes will taste. I once prepared two otherwise identical batches of soup, one with oil and the other without; no one could even tell the difference. So why add an extra five hundred calories when you don't need to? By not using oil, you will save time, money, and calories.

Another way to save time is to do batch cooking. With the Instant Pot electric pressure cooker, you can get healthy meals on the table fast. Always make sure you prepare enough food to have leftovers and snacks. If you're going to bake one potato, you might as well bake four. Leftover baked potatoes are great the next day, even served cold. It's also important to always have healthy food on hand so you won't eat crap just because you're hungry. Failing to plan means planning to fail. While canned beans are more expensive than dried beans purchased in bulk, you can buy a wide variety of salt-free canned beans at Whole Foods for under a buck per can. If you are concerned about the BPAs in the metal, you can easily find brands whose packaging is marked BPA-free.

Try inviting a friend or neighbor to join you in following an unprocessed diet; that way you can take turns making meals for each other. My friend Michelle convinced most of her colleagues to take my class, and they were inspired to eat unprocessed. Now each one of them makes lunch one day a week for the whole group. Not only do they save time, but they also get to share recipes and enjoy a wide variety of dishes. Although preparing healthy food may never be as speedy as going to a drive-through window (if there isn't a long line of cars ahead of you), it can certainly be as fast as cooking the standard American diet, even when that diet includes processed foods. In one of my YouTube videos, I show how to make decadent black bean brownies from scratch in less time than it takes to open a boxed brownie mix.

Bring green bags with you when you shop for produce. Using green bags not only helps the environment by not wasting more plastic bags, but it also saves time because you can put the items you buy directly into your refrigerator when you get home. Make a green smoothie for breakfast and drink it in the car on your way to work. You can even put the ingredients in the blender the night before so all you have to do in the morning is push a button. At Trader Joe's and many other stores you can buy reasonably priced organic produce that is often already washed and cut, which will save you considerable prep time. You can also find a variety of lettuces as well as dark leafy greens (such as kale, spinach, and collards) prewashed and cut. Many stores also sell shredded green and purple cabbage, shredded carrots, broccoli slaw, and chopped onions. You can now even find peeled garlic and prewashed leeks. These prewashed and precut foods may be more costly, however, so if you need to save money, see YABBUT #1.

With the exception of my lasagna, which is more of a celebration dish, most of my recipes can be prepped in just a few minutes and will take less than thirty minutes to cook. I once taught healthy cooking classes to students at the Braille Institute, where they were given ninety minutes to prepare a five-course meal. Although the students were blind, they had no trouble achieving that goal. In fact, almost every recipe in this book was prepared by the students in the class. Even my husband can make them!

YABBUT #3: But I can't live without my (fill in the blank).

Well, if that's truly the case, then you, my friend, are addicted. What if I told you that I could guarantee you would never have diabetes, cancer, a heart attack, or a stroke, but you could never have okra again, do you think you could cope? I would venture to say yes, because you probably are not addicted to okra. Attendance is light at the Arugula Anonymous meetings. But if I told you to give up cheese, meat, sugar, or chocolate, you would probably say you can't do that. (I will never ask you to give up chocolate, just the dairy and sugar that usually accompany it.)

I think part of the problem is that people don't like the word *addict*. It conjures up the image of a derelict in a dark alley shooting up heroin. The *Merriam-Webster Dictionary* defines addiction as "a compulsive physiological or psychological need for a habit-forming substance." (Note that *any* substance can be habit forming.) If you are not addicted to these foods, then why would it be so difficult for you to give them up? Why does even the mere idea of giving them up make you sad or anxious?

Remember this: Processed foods are designed to be addictive. How does it feel knowing you are being manipulated on a biochemical level? Not good, I would hope. Instead of lusting after processed food, try boycotting the companies that make it for attempting to control your body. Bear in mind that some food manufacturers are owned by tobacco corporations, which are true champions of addiction and another industry you might not want to support.

Imagine you're at a party where four different bowls of popcorn are served. The first bowl contains air-popped popcorn with nothing on it. The second bowl contains corn popped in oil with nothing on it. The third bowl contains corn popped in oil, with just the right amount of salt sprinkled on it. And the fourth bowl contains kettle corn, which is corn popped in oil and then sprinkled with the perfect combination of sugar and salt. Most people would choose the third or fourth bowl, and I bet you dollars to doughnuts that if I were catering the party, I would have to refill the fourth bowl the most often.

Sugar, fat, and salt work together to make food damn near irresistible, which is why it makes its appearance in just about everything you love to eat. While McDonald's French fries taste primarily of salt and fat, they also have sugar in them. The same is true of most potato chips. Even items that taste primarily sweet, such as a Cinnabon cinnamon roll, have salt added. You would be hard pressed to find any processed food (or any restaurant food, for that matter) that doesn't contain a large quantity of sugar, fat, and salt. One of the best-known advertising slogans—"Bet you can't eat just one"—was for a popular potato chip, and it hit the nail on the head. The manufacturer zeroed in on how our brain chemistry works and designed the product to exploit consumers and get them hooked.

We all have dopamine receptors in our brains. Dopamine is a neurotransmitter that is released in the brain whenever we have a pleasurable experience, whether that's having sex, taking illicit drugs, or even eating high-calorie foods like a Big Mac, fries, and a Coke (a very popular combination of sugar, fat, and salt). Unfortunately, the more calorie dense the food, the more dopamine is released, so people continue to choose these unhealthy foods to get more of a dopamine rush. This is especially true when people are feeling sad or stressed. They become habituated to this higher level of dopamine and need to eat more and more processed food laden with sugar, fat, and salt to get the same degree of pleasure. The earlier in life a person begins eating this type of food, the more difficult it is to break this cycle. In many ways, it's comparable to a heroin addict who spends all his time chasing the high he experienced when he first tried the drug. He now requires increasingly greater amounts of it, not to get high but to avoid feeling bad.

It's not possible to simply cut back on a substance you are addicted to and expect to regain your health. The only way to recover your health is to quit the substance completely. When giving up any addiction—even tobacco or coffee—you may initially feel bad. But remember, the only way out is through. There is a light at the end of the tunnel, because eventually you will feel so amazing and look so great that you won't even be able to imagine going back to the dark side. Of course, if you can't do this, that's okay too. I understand that change is difficult. Some people would rather die than change.

YABBUT #4: But my friends and family won't support me.

I'm not going to lie to you; it will be easier with the support of your loved ones. But it can be done without their support. My sister (who went from a size 14 to a size 4 in seven months after eating an unprocessed diet and also lowered her cholesterol and triglycerides to healthy levels) changed her diet completely on her own. Her husband did not want to join her. While it would be great if you had the support of all your friends and family, that just may not be a reality for you. In fact, your friends and family might do more than not support you; they may also try to undermine your efforts, especially if they are unhealthy eaters themselves. Perhaps they are afraid that if you lose weight and get well, you will abandon them. Or maybe they are worried you will put them down or ridicule them because of their food choices. It's possible they're scared you will become slim and healthy while they stay fat and sick. Or it could be that if you start acknowledging your addiction, they would be forced to acknowledge theirs. They may feel personally offended by your attempts to lead a healthier life. So, with all that in mind, my advice is for you to leave them alone. You can't change them anyway, so just work on yourself. In time, when they see the positive changes in you, they may become interested and ask you what you're doing.

When I lived in Los Angeles, I offered the "Unprocessed 30-Day Challenge" (thirty days on an unprocessed diet). Pamela, a woman in her fifties, was the first winner of the challenge. She became a size 6 and posted photos of herself on Facebook in a bikini. All her friends wanted to know what she had done to get so slim. They weren't even interested in the fact that she had lowered her cholesterol to the point where she no longer needed medication; they only cared that she looked hot!

It's interesting how when you are eating crap, no one gives a hoot (except for me!). But the minute you start eating healthfully, all of a sudden, everyone is a nutritionist, and they will come out with the most absurd and unfounded comments.

If you can, find a buddy, even if it's one online. You can join the McDougall discussion forums (drmcdougall.com) for free and also find many Meetup groups (meetup.com) dedicated to healthy eating. Most importantly, find a doctor who understands nutrition and supports the plant-based lifestyle by doing a search at pcrm.org/findadoctor or plantbaseddocs.com.

Explain to your family how important this is to you. Let them know that you want to eat a healthy diet so you'll be around a long time to take care of them and be there for them. Unfortunately, most people don't realize the consequences of their lifelong food choices until it's almost too late. Try to make it fun for them. Research shows that kids will eat what they prepare, so get them involved in the kitchen. Initiate the two-bite rule when it comes to food: They don't have to eat everything or like everything, but they have to take at least two bites of each new and unfamiliar food. Remember, their palates are as jaded as yours from years of eating processed foods, and it will take time for them to adjust. Sometimes a new food has to be offered several times and in different ways for it to be enjoyed. If you can't completely clean out your pantry, at least move their crap to the garage, a designated shelf, or a locked food safe. Ask them if they would kindly support you by eating their junk food and fast food outside the home. Hide fruits and vegetables in their food. Don't let them see you prepare the Nutrient-Rich Chocolate Smoothie (page 50), and I promise they will love it. They will never know that the Nutrient-Rich Black Bean Soup (page 100) has two pounds of greens hidden in. If you need to eat out occasionally, see page 34.

Most people do not recognize the cause-and-effect relationship between diet and health. Usually, by the time someone is diagnosed with cancer, it has been in their body for many years. Just as a smoker doesn't get lung cancer from smoking cigarettes for a week or a month, the buildup of atherosclerotic plaque in your arteries doesn't happen overnight; it occurs after years of eating a high-fat, high-cholesterol diet. My father could never make the connection between his daily angina and daily slice of kosher salami. When he died after a failed open-heart surgery, his death certificate merely stated "coronary artery disease." But as Dr. Esselstyn so eloquently says, "Heart disease need never exist, and if it does exist, it need never progress."

If other people don't understand these concepts, don't let that stop you.

YABBUT #5: It's too hard or I have too much stress.

Please reread My Story (page 1).

Why Unprocessed?

CHAPTER 3

Americans consume most of their calories from products made from deceased animals and processed foods, and they consume less than 10 percent of their calories from the optimal sources: fruits and vegetables. The one vegetable they eat most often is the potato, which would be perfectly healthy except for the fact that it is usually in the form of French fries or it's been doused in butter and sour cream or is fully loaded with cheese and bacon.

Processed foods and animal products have much in common. Unlike whole plant foods, they are lacking in fiber. Animal products contain no fiber whatsoever, and processed foods contain little to none. Fiber has few calories, is filling, and slows the rate that sugar is absorbed into the bloodstream. It also acts like little scrubbing brushes, cleaning out the colon and taking cholesterol with it. Plus, it does wonderful things for our gut microbiome. Processed foods and meat contain little to no water, making them much more calorie dense. Remember that the more calorie rich a food is, the more dopamine your brain releases, and the more you want to eat that particular food. If you aren't consuming the bulk provided by the water and fiber in whole plant food, you will need to eat many more calories to feel satisfied. We have something in our stomachs called stretch receptors that need to be activated in order for us to feel full. While it is possible to lose weight by using portion control, in the long run that won't work because we'll eventually give in to hunger. If all you eat are processed foods and animal products, you likely will have to overconsume calories in order to activate those stretch receptors and feel satiated.

Processed foods and animal products also have something else in common: They are both calorie rich and nutrient poor. In contrast, whole plant foods (with the exception of nuts and seeds) are relatively low in calories and extremely high in nutrients, especially micronutrients. Whole plant foods contain vitamins, minerals, phytochemicals, and antioxidants. These are the nutrients we need to consume in quantity if we want to prevent and reverse disease. However, they should be consumed as whole foods, not in the form of supplements. Processed foods and animal products contain no phytochemicals or antioxidants and almost no vitamins or minerals.

In addition to having stretch receptors in our stomachs, we also have nutrient receptors in our brains. We can never meet our nutrient needs by eating processed foods or animal products because they both are virtually devoid of nutrients. It is possible for people to be obese and yet be starving on a cellular level. Until their nutrient needs are met by a diet rich in whole plant foods, they will continue to overeat. Unless the majority of your calories come from nuts and seeds, it is virtually impossible for you to overconsume on a whole-food plant-based diet. Simply put, with your nutrient and calorie needs met, and your stretch receptors activated, you would be too full to eat more than your body requires.

When your caloric intake is high because of sugar, oil, flour products, or alcohol, you are more likely to gain weight and less likely to be meeting your nutrient needs.

Let's take a look now at what I dub The Evil Trinity: sugar, oil, and salt. The more of these three ingredients you eat, especially in concert with each other, the more of them you will want. Let's review them one at a time.

SUGAR

My mother used to say, "If you don't have something nice to say, say nothing at all." The American Heart Association—hardly a group of nutritional radicals—contends that we should consume no more than 5 percent of our calories from processed sweeteners. For a person consuming 2,000 calories a day, that would be 100 calories, or approximately 5 teaspoons of sugar. With the average can of soda containing at least double that amount, how can the average American stay within these guidelines? There is no upside to sugar. It provides nothing but empty calories and is devoid of nutrients. In fact, it is an anti-nutrient, which means it actually inhibits the absorption of other nutrients.

My students are always trying to convince me that their preferred form of sweetener is healthy. "But what about agave nectar, barley malt, brown rice syrup, brown sugar, sugarcane juice, coconut sugar, evaporated cane juice, fruit juice concentrate, high-fructose corn syrup, honey, maple syrup, molasses, palm sugar, yacon syrup . . .?" Unfortunately, just because a sweetener is raw, expensive, organic, or blessed by a monk in Tibet does not make it any healthier. As my mentor Dr. Alan Goldhamer says, "Just because something is less bad doesn't make it good."

Sugar is sugar is sugar is sugar. We could probably make a case for why some of these sweeteners are less bad than others, but we can't make a case for why any of them are actually healthy. In August 2010, researchers at UCLA's Jonsson Comprehensive Cancer Center revealed that it was the fructose in sugar, not the sucrose, that causes cancer cells to proliferate. Some sweeteners, such as agave nectar, are often 90 percent or more fructose, so it makes good sense to avoid those. If you are not exceeding the recommended limit of 5 teaspoons of sugar per day, then I don't think it really matters which sugar you use, bearing in mind that honey is not vegan and it should never be given to babies. (Honey contains *C. botulinum bacteria,* which can produce a toxin in a baby's large intestine and lead to a rare but serious illness known as "infant botulism.") I love how the late Jack LaLanne would say, "You wouldn't wake up your dog in the morning and give him a cup of coffee, a doughnut, and a cigarette, so why do you do that to yourself?" I always figure that if a food is not suitable for a baby or a puppy, maybe we shouldn't be eating it either.

People often ask about stevia, xylitol, or artificial sweeteners. Stevia is an herb, but unless you are buying it in its whole leaf form, it is processed. Consequently, that does not align with the aim of this book, which is to help you eliminate or greatly decrease your consumption of processed foods. If you are going to use stevia, I would suggest using the whole leaf instead of the processed white powder. When you consume sweet items like stevia, xylitol, or any of the sugar alcohols, you fuel your desire for more sweetness. In addition, these items still stimulate the release of insulin from the pancreas. Avoid artificial sweeteners, such as aspartame, like the plague. There is a lot of evidence that they are dangerous, and disruptive to your microbiome.

People will often argue that their sweetener is superior to, or at least not as bad as, white sugar. That is comparable to arguing that snorting cocaine is better than injecting heroin. It's a process known as rationalization. People aren't seeking the healthiest sweetener so they can sprinkle it on their kale. They are using the sweeteners in conjunction with other unhealthy or low-nutrient foods like flour and oil so they can bake a cake or put some in their liquid drug of choice, such as coffee or iced tea. They want me to approve of their sweetener so they can use a few cups of it in a recipe, but that's not something I will do. Remember, all sweeteners are highly processed, highly caloric, and nutrient poor. We are meant to satisfy our sweet tooth with fruit.

Of course, avoiding sugar doesn't mean you have to dump dessert altogether. You will find several scrumptious, decadent-tasting dessert recipes in this book (see pages 128–163) that are sweetened only with dates and other fruits. I assure you these will satisfy your sweet tooth and will taste as good as or better than their counterparts laden with sugar, oil, and salt. Just try the Mint Chocolate Mousse Torte (page 132) and you'll see what I mean. (If you can't have chocolate, it's just as delicious with carob.)

Keep in mind that dates are a high-sugar, low-water fruit. So even though they are a better choice, they are still quite high in calories. A deglet noor date averages about 20 calories and a medjool date about 60 calories. Nevertheless, unlike processed sweeteners, they are a whole food, which means they do contain fiber, vitamins, minerals, and antioxidants. The presence of fiber, minerals, and micronutrients in a food slows the spike of glucose in the blood and curtails free radical formation in response to a sugar load. Plus, dates taste great; they

are like nature's candy. You can also buy date sugar (basically just dehydrated, ground dates, which qualifies it as a whole food), but it does not dissolve very well, especially in hot liquids. Also, the date sugar sold in stores is typically processed with wheat flour, so if you need to avoid wheat or gluten, that wouldn't be a good option. Although gluten-free date sugar is available online, I prefer date paste and date syrup instead. You can even make these whole-food sweeteners easily and inexpensively yourself (see page 146).

Please keep in mind that even healthier treats made of whole foods are still treats. Eat them mindfully and savor every delicious bite. Think of dates as a transition food to help you get off refined sweeteners, and do not consume them if you are diabetic.

OIL

Just as all sugar is sugar, all oil is oil. Some oils may, in fact, be worse than others, but no oil is healthy. As with sugar, the only good oil is no oil! Oil is the most fattening food on the planet, weighing in at 4,000 calories per pound! For comparison, nuts and seeds are, on average, "only" 2,800 calories per pound. And chocolate, a "mere" 2,500 calories a pound. Compare these numbers to whole plant foods, such as fruits and vegetables, which are typically 100 to 300 calories per pound. Or to potatoes, beans, and grains, which range from 400 to 600 calories per pound. Even avocados are only 750 calories a pound. For the calories in merely 1 tablespoon of olive oil, you could consume almost an entire avocado! Which do you think tastes better, would fill up your tummy, and satisfy you more? And don't forget, all oils are essentially devoid of nutrients!

People regularly tell me that they have read or heard that olive oil is heart healthy, and they never fail to mention that a study was done proving the benefits of a Mediterranean diet. However, if you take a close look at the actual research, you will find that the people studied lived on the Island of Crete in the 1950s and were healthy *in spite of* their consumption of olive oil, not *because* of it. They were also eating large quantities of fruits and vegetables and walking many miles a day. It is true that if you switch from using butter to using olive oil, your cholesterol may go down. But take someone like me, with a blood cholesterol of 90–110 mg/dl. If I were to start eating oil, my cholesterol would go up! Also, if you read the label on a bottle of oil, you'll see that the recommended serving size is 1 tablespoon. How many people do you know who eat only 1 tablespoon of oil per day? The average person will drench an otherwise healthy salad or vegetable dish with at least 400 calories of pure fat. For that many calories, you could eat 4 pounds of salad, 1 pound of sweet potatoes, or almost 2 pounds of fruit. Which do you think will fill you up and satisfy you more? Coconut oil, at 92 percent saturated fat (the worst kind of fat), is the most dangerous of all and has more saturated fat than even meat!

It is very easy to prepare delicious food without oil. As with salt, in most cases you can simply omit it. Except for frying (and we shouldn't be eating fried foods anyway), any recipe that calls for oil can be made without it; I bet you won't even notice the difference. Air fryers, which are now readily available, can create foods that mimic the texture of fried foods without using oil. If you need to sauté, you can use any liquid: water, fruit juice, vegetable juice, or salt-free vegetable broth all work well. Just make sure you have a good nonstick pan and add only a small amount of the liquid at a time. Watch closely and stir almost constantly so the food in the pan doesn't burn. You can even caramelize onions in the oven without oil.

When I adapt dessert recipes, I often use applesauce in place of oil or coconut meat in place of coconut oil. When I roast vegetables in the oven, I use high-quality balsamic vinegar instead of oil.

Maybe you're still not convinced. After all, popular TV personalities, such as Dr. Oz and Rachael Ray, say that olive oil is heart healthy. There's a lot of misinformation floating about, so let me explain it to you this way: Suppose there is something truly beneficial in olive oil, coconut oil, or flax oil. Wouldn't it follow, then, that the beneficial something would also be in the whole-food form—that is, in olives, coconuts, and flaxseeds—not just their oils? Are we supposed to believe that something magically happens during the processing of oil that somehow adds these beneficial compounds that were not present in the whole food to begin with?

I hope this is starting to make sense. When you take olives and make olive oil, pretty much everything good about the olive (such as the fiber, vitamins, and

minerals) is processed out and all that remains is sludge. When food is processed, it becomes calorie rich and nutrient poor. I want you to eat unprocessed whole foods. No oil is a whole food; all oils are highly processed. So, eat the olive, not the olive oil. Eat whole coconut (in moderation), never coconut oil. And eat ground whole flaxseeds, not flax oil. You would be absolutely amazed at how much weight you could lose even if oil were the only thing you took out of your diet.

Keep in mind that when I'm cautioning you about oil, I am not telling you to avoid eating fat. I am telling you that when you do eat fat, make sure it's in the whole-food form, as with nuts, seeds, and avocado, and eat these foods in moderation. Always have nuts and seeds that are raw, not roasted, and unsalted. Kids need fat, but they don't need oil. They can get all the fat their brains need from avocado, nuts, seeds, and unsalted nut and seed butters. You can even occasionally indulge in rich, high-fat plant foods, such as tofu and tempeh. Yes, they are minimally processed, so if you want to be a purist, just go back to the whole-food source and eat edamame. Edamame in the shell make a delicious and fun snack. Soy and corn are two of the most genetically modified crops, so if you are worried about consuming GMOs, make sure you read the label and get a non-GMO brand. I don't recommend most of the vegan meat and cheese substitutes. The majority of them are highly processed and loaded with oil and salt. Isolated soy protein, which is found in many of the vegan meats, has been shown to be harmful. While it's true that, unlike animal products, vegan meats have no cholesterol and may be a good transition food, the goal is to be eating whole, unprocessed plant foods.

Dr. McDougall, whom I have long admired, generally recommends that we should get no more than 10 percent of our calories from fat. He points out that nuts, seeds, avocado, and other high-fat plant foods are condiments and occasional treats that should only be eaten if we are not overweight. Many of his colleagues agree with him. Dr. Esselstyn, another hero of mine, says if you have heart disease and your LDL is above 80 mg/dl, you should avoid nuts, seeds, and avocado. Our dinners almost always consist of potatoes of one color or another (in honor of Dr. McDougall) and a massive quantity of steamed greens à la Esselstyn. At my last annual physical, my LDL was 71 mg/dl, and I don't eat nuts, seeds, or avocado.

I don't think that whole-food fats are evil or inherently unhealthy, but I know that when I consumed them, I could not maintain the ideal weight that I maintain now. My best advice is this: Eat the least restrictive plant-exclusive diet that will get you the results you seek. For me, that diet does not include nuts, seeds, or avocado. If you're worried about your omega-3 fatty acids, I recommend a tablespoon of ground flaxseeds or chia seeds daily.

I like to look at what all the plant-based experts agree on. Basically, they all say we should be eating a whole-food plant-based diet with no oil, little or no processed sugar, and little or no salt. If everyone did that, disease rates would plummet.

SALT

But we need salt. Isn't sea salt good for you? If I had a nickel for every time I heard these comments, I would be a rich woman. Yes, we require a small amount of sodium, but we can be healthy with as little as 150 milligrams per day. One teaspoon of salt has 2,325 milligrams of sodium, and we require merely one-sixteenth of a teaspoon a day for bodily functions. How many people add only one-sixteenth of a teaspoon of salt a day to their food? The recommended ceiling for sodium is no more than 2,300 milligrams per day. If you are eating any processed food at all, you definitely are not sodium deficient. How many people do you know who are actually deficient in sodium? In addition to raising your blood pressure, high salt consumption is also linked to stroke and stomach cancer and acts as an appetite stimulant.

The more salt you eat, the more salt you crave. When you are addicted to salt, you can't really appreciate the amazing flavors in whole foods. Have you ever heard that when people quit smoking they gain weight? While there are many factors that contribute to this occurrence, I believe one is that when former smokers no longer singe their taste buds with hot tobacco, they can more fully taste and enjoy food again. The same is true when people give up salt. Once the palate adjusts, the inherent saltiness in whole foods comes through loud and clear. Just as when people stop consuming processed sweeteners and fruit suddenly tastes exceedingly sweet, a similar change happens when they forgo salt. Even celery will taste salty! My taste buds are so clean now that I can eat a plain baked potato topped with steamed broccoli and no seasonings, including no salt, and truly enjoy it! Even products labeled "low sodium" can still be fairly high in sodium. Sometimes they even contain MSG. I used to use low-sodium vegetable broth when making soups, but I found they were still too high in sodium. Plus, why should I pay three bucks a carton when water is free? Not flavorful enough for you? You can make your own veggie broth or use fresh vegetable juice, or a combination of juices, as a base. Fresh celery, carrot, and tomato juices are my favorites.

If you still crave a salty taste, there are a few things you can use to simulate that flavor. First, I would recommend eating sea vegetables. There are several varieties—such as kelp, dulse, nori, and kombu—that can be purchased in whole sheets. (It's long been said that if beans are cooked with a piece of kombu, they won't promote gas.) Smoked dulse is my favorite, and I love using chopped pieces of it in salads and oil-free stir-fries. Some sea veggies, primarily kelp and dulse, are available granulated or powdered, so you can sprinkle them on foods just as you would salt. Sea vegetables are harvested from the ocean, so they are high in minerals and have a naturally salty taste with a fraction of the sodium (roughly 25 to 35 milligrams per teaspoon) of salt.

You can buy sea vegetables at most natural food stores, but you will find better prices online at seaveg.com. Several salt-free seasoning blends can be found at almost any grocery store. I am not advocating salt substitutes that contain potassium chloride; rather, I'm referring to natural salt-free blends or dried herbs and spices. Please visit ChefAJ.com to see some of my favorite SOS-free seasonings.

When I worked at the retirement home, the chefs were prohibited from using any salt or salt substitutes. Instead, they made their food pop with flavor by using plenty of spices, including garlic, cumin, and pepper, as well as lots of fresh herbs, such as parsley, basil, thyme, rosemary, and cilantro, just to name a few. You can always use dried herbs, but in my opinion, fresh tastes best. Adding both the juice and zest from lemons or limes to the finish of your soups and stews and to salad dressings also tricks the palate into thinking there is salt in the dish.

Now it's time for me to bring out the big guns: sun-dried tomatoes. I simply put them in my high-powered blender and turn them into a coarse powder, which is extraordinarily rich and flavorful and something I use in many of my recipes. If you don't have a high-powered blender, you can grind them in a small electric coffee grinder, which you can purchase for less than twenty bucks. Just make sure you don't overfill the unit. Use only oil-free sun-dried tomatoes, the kind that is usually found in cellophane bags in the produce section of stores. They are on the firmer, drier side. This technique will not work with oil-packed

sun-dried tomatoes, as they will turn into a paste, not a powder. Even many regular grocery stores sell bulk sun-dried tomatoes in the produce section. You can also find sun-dried tomato powder in many spice stores or online. It takes four pounds of fresh tomatoes to make just three ounces of sun-dried tomatoes, which is why they're so flavorful. Of course, if you have a food dehydrator, you can easily make your own sun-dried tomatoes.

But what about the expensive designer salts, like Celtic sea salt or pink Himalayan salt? They have minerals, don't they? Although there is a negligible amount of minerals in sea salt compared to iodized salt, no one eats salt to obtain minerals; that's what green vegetables are for! To avoid iodine deficiency, eat sea vegetables or ask your doctor if you should occasionally take an iodine supplement.

If you are used to a high-sodium diet, some of the recipes in this book may taste bland to you for a while, so here are a few secrets I employ when I'm entertaining "regular people." Instead of salt, I will use either low-sodium miso or coconut aminos. Miso, a fermented food used in Japan for centuries to make soup, may have only 110 milligrams of sodium per teaspoon, depending on the brand and type of miso you purchase. (That's the amount in the brand I buy; others can be much, much higher, so always read the label!) Compare 110 milligrams per teaspoon of miso to 2,300 milligrams per teaspoon of salt. You can have almost twenty-four teaspoons of miso for the same amount of sodium, and miso is a rich paste that tastes very salty, so you end up using far less of it than you would table salt. When I was in Japan, we had miso soup for breakfast every morning, as the Japanese believe it has many health benefits. Tamari is basically soy sauce that is wheat free, which is preferable for people who must avoid wheat. Low-sodium tamari has 700 milligrams of sodium per tablespoon, roughly 233 milligrams of sodium per teaspoon, which is still way less than the 2,300 milligrams in a teaspoon of salt. Trader Joe's low-sodium soy sauce (which is not wheat-free) contains only 460 milligrams of sodium per tablespoon, roughly 153 milligrams of sodium per teaspoon, which is still a far cry from the 2,300 milligrams in a teaspoon of salt. Even better, coconut aminos will take the place of soy sauce and contains only 90 milligrams of sodium per teaspoon.

Remember, if you still insist on using salt, at least don't cook with it. Add it judiciously to the surface of your food where the taste buds on the tip of your tongue can readily taste it. But first see if you can skip the salt altogether, especially if you already have high blood pressure or want to lose weight.

Getting Started

CHAPTER 4

THE POSSIBILITY OF A NEW YOU

My first recommendation is that you experiment with an unprocessed diet for just thirty days to assess how you feel, knowing that at the end of the thirty days you can go back to eating whatever you want. Compare how you feel while eating unprocessed whole foods to how you felt eating a processed food diet. I have never had one person come back and tell me that, after the initial period of detox and withdrawal, he or she actually felt better eating processed food.

I recommend the thirty-day trial period because people can become anxious and afraid when they believe something is going to last forever. I know that's what happened to me when I tried to give up my former addiction, chocolate. It was the worst month of my husband's life! So don't even think about doing this for thirty days if that causes you too much anxiety. Think of doing it a day at a time, a meal at a time, or even a bite at a time. Instead of thinking about what you are giving up, think about what you are moving towards.

People often make fun of me for eating this way, with little jabs like, "You're really not going to live any longer; it will just *seem longer*." But the truth is that I actually *prefer* eating this way. I love rarely having to go to the doctor. I love almost never getting sick. I love not having to take dangerous, expensive, ineffective medications to lower my blood pressure, cholesterol, or blood sugar—drugs that often, in the end, only make people sicker. Think about what your quality of life could be if you improve your health. Think about being around to walk your son or daughter down the aisle or being alive for the birth of your first grandchild.

So, are you starting to see the possibility of a new you? Are you starting to get excited? Then let's talk about how to begin. The first thing I recommend is to clean out all the crap from your cabinets and refrigerator. I've sometimes helped people do this as they cry and scream. Usually once I clean out someone's kitchen, there is nothing left that I would consider food, so I take them shopping.

You need to get rid of all processed food. I define processed food as pretty much anything that comes in a can, box, bottle, or bag. If it's not a whole food, then it's a processed food. All oils, sugars, and alcohols are processed. Generally, if an item has more than just a few ingredients, it's processed. I do make an exception for sugar-free, low-sodium condiments, such as ketchup and mustard, as well as salt-free canned beans and unsweetened nondairy milks without added sugar or oil. You actually can make these milks easily yourself but keeping some packaged ones on hand is fine.

Once you truly understand that processed food is not food, this way of eating will be so much easier. You may love processed food or be addicted to it, or perhaps you may choose to eat it (only occasionally I hope). Nevertheless, it is not food. Most of what Americans eat—most of what you'll find in a grocery store—is readily available, socially acceptable, and affordable, but it is neither whole nor food.

There is a popular vegan restaurant in Los Angeles called Real Food Daily. I love that name because people need to learn that they must eat real food and eat it daily. You must eat food, whole food, and nothing but the whole food. A whole food is something that comes to our kitchen as grown. Since most of us don't grow our own food, think of a whole food as basically anything you can find in the produce section of the grocery store. If it's not a fruit, vegetable (starchy or non-starchy), whole grain, legume, nut, or seed, then it's not a whole food; it's a processed food.

Trust me, you don't want processed crap around you, tempting you and contaminating the good food you are about to bring into your home. Think of it like bringing home a newborn baby. You'd make sure everything was spotless first, wouldn't you? If you are going to eat "off plan," do so only *outside* of your home. Never have these foods *in* your home, as the temptation will be too great. If there's crappy food in your house, it will sing to you and you will eat it! Please do not think you can rely on willpower alone. Don't sabotage yourself. If you were a recovering alcoholic, would you get a job at a bar? Of course not! All non-food items must be consumed outside of your home. If you have to leave your home to eat them, you will become infinitely more aware of your addictive patterns and mindless eating. Eat mindfully. And if you do fall off the wagon, get right back on with the very next bite of food you put into your mouth.

Now that you know the rules, it's time to play the game. Let's go shopping. Let's start in the produce section, where the sky's the limit. Buy whatever looks good to you. I often buy what appeals to me visually, such as rainbow chard or purple kale. But I also use my nose, especially with fruit, and buy whatever smells good. You can also ask one of the produce people for help with selecting the ripest fruits. Although you can buy fresh fruit that's been pre-cut, it will be more expensive. Make sure you purchase plenty of ripe bananas; they freeze well are great in smoothies and for making ice cream.

Since there is no limit to the amount of fruits and vegetables you're permitted to eat, buy as much as you think you will be able to consume until the next time you can go shopping. Make sure you buy some citrus fruits, such as lemons, limes, and oranges. They are great for squeezing over a salad, making oil-free dressings, and using in many of the recipes in this book. "Eat the rainbow" and buy vegetables of every color, such as red bell pepper, yellow squash, and purple cabbage. I love putting shredded raw beets in my salads. You will also want to buy sun-dried tomatoes, which are usually located in the produce section. Make sure you get the kind that are oil-free and salt-free and have no sulfites added. Sulfites are a preservative that many people (including me) are allergic to. Sulfites can even trigger migraine headaches and asthma attacks. Make sure you buy ample starches, such as potatoes or sweet potatoes of any color, whole grains, and legumes (which includes beans, split peas, and lentils). Most of what you will buy and eat will be from the produce section, so be very careful if you venture out to the rest of the store unattended.

Next, go to the frozen-food section and buy frozen fruit for smoothies or desserts. My favorite is frozen cherries. Make sure the fruits don't have sugar added. Also stock up on your favorite frozen vegetables. If you don't think you will make your own nondairy milk, or if you want to have prepared nondairy milk on hand in case of an emergency, buy a few boxes. Cashew milk is my favorite, but if you are allergic to nuts, look for hemp milk, rice milk, soy milk, or oat milk. Most brands will have added sodium, so if you want to be a purist, make your own using my recipe for Almond Milk (page 41).

I want you to love your salads, so it's critical that your dressing is delicious. Some whole-food mixtures that make great dressings are oil-free hummus (see Creamy Hummus, page 57, and Hummus Dressing, page 94), guacamole (see Sweet Pea Guacamole, page 61), and Pico de Gallo (page 124).

Finally, end your healthy shopping trip with a visit to the bulk section and buy your favorite beans and grains.

Quinoa (which is technically a seed, not a grain) and millet are my favorites, but you can also choose oats, rice, buckwheat, and a plethora of other whole grains. Most grains sold in bulk are also available in boxes. Boxed whole grains are more expensive, but if you've never cooked whole grains before, they're a great way to start out because the directions will be on the package. If you don't want to cook dried beans, look for salt-free beans in a can. Even if you do cook dried beans, the canned ones are good to have on hand.

Feel free to browse the spice aisle and buy any spices or extracts that tickle your fancy. Also seek out fresh herbs in the produce section. Make sure you have a supply of flaxseeds or chia seeds so that you can put a tablespoon in your smoothies or on your salads to get all your essential fatty acids. Flaxseeds must be ground first in order for the body to assimilate them, so if you don't have a coffee grinder or blender, you can always buy them already ground. Just be sure to keep them in the refrigerator, as the ground seeds can quickly become rancid.

What about alcohol, you ask? Well, from a nutrition standpoint, it's like oil and sugar; alcohol has no nutrients, just calories. And it is almost twice as fattening as sugar and almost as fattening as oil. Sugar has four calories per gram; alcohol has seven calories per gram; and oil has nine calories per gram. In addition, most people eat more when they are drinking alcoholic beverages, and usually that means more unhealthy foods. Sure, you may occasionally hear about a study that attributes some health benefit to alcohol consumed in moderation. But as with oil, if there truly is something beneficial in wine, it's also in the grapes the wine was made from. So, again, eat the whole food! The answer is always in the whole food.

If you still drink coffee, which I know can be hard to give up, you might not want to even think about stopping it until you have superior nutrition under your belt for several months. Many people enrolled in the "Unprocessed 30-Day Challenge" with the goal of eliminating caffeine, which they met with success. Remember, coffee is a drug, so you may need some help to come off it. Try drinking your regular coffee with half decaf for a while until you can titrate down to the lowest dose. If you still need the caffeine, switch to green tea, a healthier choice; but if you don't need the caffeine, keep in mind that you can get all the health benefits of green tea in its decaffeinated form.

The only beverages I recommend are water and herbal teas. Just as human beings are the only species to drink milk after maturity and are the only species to drink the lactation fluids of another mammal, we also are the only species to drink, after maturity, any beverage other than water. You may have heard that the amount of water you should drink is half of your weight in ounces. However, if you are eating water-rich foods like fruits and vegetables, you may not need that much. Caffeine is dehydrating, so if you are still consuming it, you will need to drink even more water. Once you are thirsty, you are already dehydrated, so make sure you never reach that point. And always adjust your fluid intake according to the weather and the amount of exercise you do. I really don't recommend drinking juices unless they are freshly squeezed vegetable juices. And never, ever drink liquid meat (aka dairy). Cow's milk was made for a baby calf to grow to 800 pounds in one year. It is not fit for human consumption. Milk does a body no good.

EATING OUT

t is hard enough eating out on a plant-based diet, let alone a whole-food plant-based diet free of sugar, salt, and oil, but it can be done. For starters, let's talk a little bit about restaurants. Please keep in mind that, like the processed food industry, restaurants are in business to make a profit. Remember, the more salt in food, the more of that food you will eat. Not surprisingly, restaurants use more salt than you could imagine. Way more salt than you would ever cook with at home. So unless you are ordering a plain salad, a plain baked potato, steamed vegetables, or fresh fruit, the likelihood of getting a salt-free or even-reduced sodium meal at a restaurant is slim to none. If you ask chefs to prepare food without salt, they will look at you as if you have three heads. It's not their fault. Culinary schools don't teach their students how to prepare food salt-free. Even if they did, the vast majority of people who frequent restaurants either do not eat this way or do not expect to when they dine out. So know that when you eat out you are probably going to ingest way more sodium than you would want. Just like the processed food industry, restaurants also use the perfect combination of sugar, fat, and salt to keep you coming back for more. And the portion size at many restaurants (like Cheesecake Factory and Chili's) is enough to feed a family of four.

The same goes for oil. Since the majority of the public still believes all the hype about olive oil being "good for your heart," and since chefs don't learn to cook without it in culinary school, pretty much everything in a restaurant is cooked in or with oil. Most food in a restaurant is prepped in advance and is not cooked to order. Again, if you order nothing but the four items I suggested above (a plain salad, a plain baked potato, steamed vegetables, or fresh fruit), you won't even have to worry about oil. But if you want something a bit more exciting, my advice is to call the restaurant ahead of time and ask them if the chef can accommodate your special dietary needs. Almost all restaurants have their menus online now, so you can look them up and see what dishes look good to you. Then call the restaurant during non-peak hours and ask if they can be of service. Please don't wait until you arrive and the restaurant is already busy and crowded. Many chefs are happy to accommodate customers with a bit of advance notice.

The first homework assignment for participants in our "Unprocessed 30-Day Challenge" was to go online and look up the nutritional information for one of the restaurants they frequent and highlight what they usually order. When people actually see the amount of saturated fat, calories, and sodium in their food choices, they often make better selections. All chain restaurants are required to have this information available. You will generally have better luck at restaurants that allow you to customize your meal. Seek out restaurants where you can eat simple ingredients, like a plant-exclusive meal at a poke bowl restaurant or a simple salad at a salad bar restaurant. At some restaurants, the best you may be able to do is to order a baked potato.

At Chinese restaurants, you can always get steamed rice and steamed veggies. You can request that no oil be used, but there's no guarantee they will comply. Many restaurants are really making an effort to provide healthier options. Sharky's, a Mexican fast-food restaurant on the West Coast, offers organic low-fat whole-wheat tortillas, organic brown rice, and organic pinto beans; they even offer the Chef AJ Burrito, Bowl, and Plate! You can even get my favorite, steamed broccoli, on your burrito! And they have an exquisite fire-roasted salsa! Hugo's restaurant, with several locations in Southern California, has a large number of healthier options on their menu. So change is happening, albeit slowly. I know of only two restaurants that cook without sugar, oil, and salt: Casa de Luz in Austin, Texas, and GreenFare restaurant in Herndon, Virginia.

My friend Shayda's journey of losing 120 pounds and getting off all her medications began by taking my Unprocessed 30-Day Challenge. Mark lost 20 pounds, lowered his cholesterol by 70 points, completely reversed his type 2 diabetes, and was able to discontinue his medication. Wolfie lost 40 pounds and started wearing pants without an elastic waist. Pamela had been told by her doctor that she would have to go on statins; instead she went on the Challenge, lost 20 pounds, and got her cholesterol under 150 mg/dl. Stacie got off sugar, caffeine, and alcohol. My sister, Barbara, went from a size 14 to a size 4 in seven months and got her cholesterol and triglycerides within normal limits. The list goes on and on. I don't know anyone who has regretted trying an unprocessed diet.

Keep in mind that these common diseases caused by our poor food choices are far easier to prevent than they are to treat. But many of them can be reversed, and it's only too late if you don't start now. Although our culture isn't geared toward healthy eating, more and more people are willing to offer support. Still, changing your diet is largely something you must do for yourself, by yourself. Try eating unprocessed for just thirty days and see how you feel. What you will experience in terms of increased energy, vitality, and improved health will far outweigh any inconvenience. The staff at Optimum Health Institute often said, "Just do your best and bless the rest." Good advice.

I hope reading my story has inspired you to make some changes in the direction of optimum health. If you'd like more information, you can find it at ChefAJ.com; you also can connect with me there. William Jennings Bryan once said, "Never be afraid to stand with the minority when the minority is right, for the minority which is right will one day be the majority."

Welcome to the minority.

Love & Kale,
Chef AJ

The Recipes

CHAPTER 5

INGREDIENTS AND EQUIPMENT

The majority of ingredients you'll need to make the recipes in this book can be found in the fruit and vegetable aisle of your local supermarket or natural food store. You will also need a variety of whole grains, raw nuts and seeds, unsweetened dried fruits, frozen fruits and vegetables, unsalted canned beans, and a wide range of ground spices and seasonings.

Essential to many of my recipes is California Balsamic brand vinegar in a variety of flavors. These you will have to order online, but it will be well worth it. Just go to californiabalsamic.com. You can purchase full bottles as well as get the Chef AJ sampler to try some of my favorites. Be sure to check out my website (ChefAJ.com) for discount codes and more.

The most important equipment you'll need, in addition to standard kitchen tools and appliances, are a high-powered blender and a food processor. I also recommend getting an air fryer, so you can make crispy foods without oil, and an Instant Pot pressure cooker. Again, visit my website (ChefAJ.com) for discount codes and to learn which products and brands are my favorites.

LET'S GET COOKING!

One of the best things about eating an unprocessed, oil-free, sugar-free, salt-free, nutrient-rich, whole-food, plant-based diet is that unless you are overdoing the whole-food fats—such as avocado, coconut, nuts, seeds—you can pretty much eat all the food you desire. That is why we elected not to include the serving sizes and nutritional information in the recipe section. When you are eating exclusively fruits, vegetables, whole grains, and legumes every day, there is no need to count calories or weigh or measure your food. An ounce of nuts or seeds per day is fine, but only if they don't unfavorably affect your weight. If you eat when you are hungry, stop when you are full, and don't eat animal products or refined and processed food (or, if you must, keep their intake to less than 10 percent of your total calories), you will no longer be obsessed with counting anything.

Of course, exercise is important. But you can't outrun a bad diet (although you sure can supercharge a good one). With these recipes, we know that you will be able to enjoy food that comes from plants instead of a manufacturing plant.

For this 10th anniversary edition of *Unprocessed,* I've added over thirty new recipes, listed below so you can easily find them:

APPETIZERS AND SIDES

BEVERAGES

BREAKFASTS

beverages & breakfasts

40

Almond Milk

Why buy plant milk in a box laden with sodium when you can make your own for just pennies a glass?

1 cup raw ALMONDS or your favorite nuts or seeds

Soak the almonds overnight in water. Be sure to cover the almonds completely, as they will expand as they absorb the water. In the morning, drain the almonds completely and rinse them well several times. Put the almonds in a high-powered blender with 3 cups water. Blend on high speed until the almonds are fully incorporated into the liquid. Pour the mixture into a nut milk bag or a paint straining bag over a bowl until you can't squeeze any more liquid out of the pulp. Refrigerate any unused milk. The milk will keep for 2 to 3 days.

CHEF'S NOTES: Use a new paint straining bag, not one that's been used for painting! You can get these at any hardware store or online for about a buck.

If you like a thicker, richer nut milk that is more like cream, just add less water. For thinner almond milk, add more water.

You can reserve the pulp for another use, such as making cookies or crackers.

CHEAP AND EASY ALMOND MILK: Put 1 tablespoon of raw almond butter in a blender with 3 cups water and process until smooth.

SWEET ALMOND MILK: Add pitted dates, to taste, and 1 tablespoon alcohol-free vanilla extract or 1 teaspoon vanilla powder. (The vanilla is optional but good.)

Zucchini Milk

NEW!

A great way to sneak in more veggies!

ZUCCHINI

Put zucchini in a high-powered blender and process until smooth.

> **CHEF'S NOTES:** This can be used in baked dishes as well as soup recipes that call for milk.

Cinnamon Bun Milk

NEW!

A splash of this is delicious in hot tea (I drink vanilla tea), and I bet it would be a great substitute for coffee creamer. This tastes like a classic Cinnabon cinnamon roll!

½ cup raw **PECANS**

½ cup **ROLLED OATS**

⅓ cup **GOLDEN RAISINS**

2 large medjool **DATES**, pitted

1 teaspoon **GROUND CINNAMON**

1 teaspoon **VANILLA POWDER**

Put all the ingredients in a NutraMilk machine on the "Butter" cycle for 2 minutes. Add 4 cups of water and press "Mix." The machine will run for 1 minute. Press "Dispense." If you don't have a NutraMilk machine, put all the ingredients in a high-powered blender and process until smooth and creamy. Strain through a nut milk or paint straining bag. Store the milk in the refrigerator.

Piña Colada Milk NEW!

1 cup raw **CASHEWS**

1 cup **DRIED PINEAPPLE**

¼ cup reduced-fat **COCONUT FLAKES** (see Chef's Notes)

Put all the ingredients in a NutraMilk machine on the "Butter" cycle for 2 minutes. Add 4 cups of water and press "Mix." The machine will run for 1 minute. Press "Dispense." If you don't have a NutraMilk machine, put all the ingredients in a high-powered blender and process until smooth and creamy. Strain through a nut milk or paint straining bag. Store the milk in the refrigerator.

CHEF'S NOTES: Reduced-fat coconut is available at many natural grocery stores and online.

To turn this into a smoothie, add 1 to 2 frozen bananas and process until smooth.

Pistachio Milk

Although you can buy pistachio milk in stores, it's easy to make your own.

2 cups raw **PISTACHIOS**

Soak the pistachios in water for several hours. Drain and rinse well. Transfer to a high-powered blender. Add 2 cups water and process on high. Pour through a nut milk bag or a paint straining bag over a bowl and gently squeeze to separate the pulp from the milk. Store leftover milk in the refrigerator.

CHEF'S NOTE: Use a little more water for a thinner, lighter milk.

Mint Chocolate Chip Smoothie

Looks and tastes like mint chocolate-chip ice cream!

1 cup **PISTACHIO MILK** (page 43)

1 frozen **BANANA**

Pitted **DATES**, to taste

1 tablespoon alcohol-free **VANILLA EXTRACT**, or 1 teaspoon **VANILLA POWDER**

20 **FRESH MINT** leaves, or to taste

3 large **KALE** leaves

ICE cubes

Handful **CACAO** nibs

Put the milk, banana, dates, vanilla extract, mint leaves, kale leaves, and ice cubes in a high-powered blender and process until smooth. Add the nibs and pulse briefly.

It's Easy Being Green Smoothie

I always serve this in my cooking classes, and even people who think they hate greens love it.

2 cups freshly squeezed **ORANGE JUICE**, or 2 to 3 peeled **ORANGES**

1 bunch **KALE** (about 12 ounces) **or SPINACH**

2 frozen **BANANAS**

2 cups frozen **MANGO** chunks

FRESH MINT leaves, to taste (optional)

Put the kale and orange juice or oranges in a high-powered blender and process until smooth. Add the bananas, mango, and mint and process until smooth and thick.

CHEF'S NOTES: You can also use 1 cup unsweetened almond milk plus 1 cup freshly squeezed orange juice for the liquid.

Guilt-Free Frappuccino   *NEW!*

A small Frappuccino at Starbucks has 350 calories, 44 grams of sugar, and 17 grams of fat! My version contains virtually no fat and has a fraction of the calories, and the only sugar comes from fruit.

2 large frozen **BANANAS**

1 cup unsweetened **NONDAIRY MILK**

3 to 4 large medjool **DATES, pitted** (depending on how sweet you like it)

¼ cup **ROLLED OATS**

1½ tablespoons Sei Mee Roasted **BROWN RICE COFFEE,** or 2 tablespoons Dandy Blend or other **HERBAL COFFEE SUBSTITUTE**

1 teaspoon **CHIA** seeds

1 teaspoon **VANILLA POWDER**

½ teaspoon **GROUND CINNAMON**

⅛ teaspoon **GROUND NUTMEG**

Put all the ingredients in a high-powered blender and blend until smooth and creamy. For a thicker shake, add ice cubes after the other ingredients have been blended and process until the desired thickness is achieved.

CHEF'S NOTES: When I worked at the TrueNorth Health Center, we were not permitted to use either regular vanilla extract (since it contains alcohol) or alcohol-free vanilla extract (since it contains glycerin). Using whole vanilla beans is extremely expensive, so I began using vanilla powder. It made such a difference in flavor that I simply could not go back to using the inferior extracts. For this recipe, the vanilla powder is essential in order to achieve the authentic flavor of the date shakes of the desert. If you can't find pure vanilla powder in grocery stores, you'll find it on Amazon.

To make fudgesicles, pour the mixture into popsicle molds and freeze.

Chocolate-Covered Cherry Smoothie

This smoothie's pretty shade of pink reminds me of a cherry cordial.

2 cups frozen **CHERRIES**

1½ cups unsweetened **CHOCOLATE ALMOND MILK**

1 frozen **BANANA**

2 tablespoons unsweetened **COCOA POWDER** or **CAROB POWDER**

2 tablespoons unsweetened **CHERRY BUTTER**

Pitted **DATES**, to taste

ICE cubes

1 to 2 tablespoons **CACAO** nibs

Put the cherries, almond milk, banana, cocoa powder, cherry butter, dates, and ice cubes in a high-powered blender and process until smooth. Add the nibs and pulse briefly.

Caramel Fakiatto

A small amount of caramel extract really gives this rich, creamy treat that *je ne sais quoi*.

1 cup unsweetened **CHOCOLATE ALMOND MILK**

2 tablespoons unsweetened **COCOA POWDER** or **CAROB POWDER**

1 large frozen **BANANA**

Pitted **DATES**, to taste

12 **ICE** cubes, plus more as needed to reach desired thickness

½ teaspoon **CARAMEL EXTRACT**

Put all the ingredients in a high-powered blender and process until thick and smooth. Don't share!

CHEF'S NOTES: We use Watkins Caramel Extract, available in many stores and on Amazon

Apple Pie Smoothie

Tastes like apple pie in a glass!

2 cups frozen **PEACHES**

1 frozen **BANANA**

1½ cups unsweetened **ALMOND MILK**

½ cup unsweetened **APPLE BUTTER**

Pitted **DATES**, to taste

1 tablespoon alcohol-free **VANILLA EXTRACT**, or 1 teaspoon **VANILLA POWDER**

1 teaspoon **GROUND CINNAMON**

¼ teaspoon **GROUND NUTMEG**

ICE cubes

Put all the ingredients in a high-powered blender and process until smooth.

CHEF'S NOTES: If you can't find apple butter, try substituting unsweetened apple juice for all or part of the almond milk.

Pumpkin Pie Smoothie

Tastes like pumpkin pie in a glass.

2 cups unsweetened nondairy **MILK**

1 (15-ounce) can **PUMPKIN** (not pumpkin pie filling)

2 frozen **BANANAS**

Pitted **DATES**, to taste

1 tablespoon **PUMPKIN PIE SPICE**

1 tablespoon alcohol-free **VANILLA EXTRACT**, or 1 teaspoon **VANILLA POWDER**

ICE cubes

Put all the ingredients in a high-powered blender and process until smooth.

The Incredible Hulk

I love the vibrant green color of this juice.

>   1 bunch **KALE** (about 12 ounces)
>
>   2 **APPLES**
>
>   1 **CUCUMBER**
>
>   Juice of 1 **LIME**

Put all the ingredients through a juicer. Enjoy immediately.

> **CHEF'S NOTES:** I prefer green smoothies rather than juice because the smoothies include healthy pulp and fiber from the veggies and fruit.
>
> Citrus fruits must either be peeled first before putting through a juicer or squeezed separately.

Vanilla Shake

Serve in a milkshake glass for a classic vanilla shake.

>   1 frozen **BANANA**
>
>   1 cup unsweetened **ALMOND MILK**
>
>   Pitted **DATES**, to taste
>
>   1 tablespoon alcohol-free **VANILLA EXTRACT**, or 1 teaspoon **VANILLA POWDER**
>
>   **ICE** cubes

Put all the ingredients in a high-powered blender and process until smooth.

> **CHEF'S NOTES:** Add 2 tablespoons cacao nibs prior to blending for a cookies and cream shake.

Nutrient-Rich Chocolate Smoothie

No one will know there are greens in this smoothie unless you tell them.

2 cups frozen **BLUEBERRIES**

¾ cup unsweetened nondairy **MILK**

½ cup **POMEGRANATE JUICE**

6 ounces organic **BABY SPINACH**

1 frozen **BANANA**

4 pitted **DATES**, more or less, to taste

3 tablespoons unsweetened **COCOA POWDER** or **CAROB POWDER**

1 tablespoon **GROUND FLAXSEEDS**

Put all the ingredients in a high-powered blender and process until smooth.

CHEF'S NOTES: This smoothie is also delicious without the dates and cocoa powder.

Fruity Quinoa

A great change of pace from your morning oatmeal.

½ cup **QUINOA**

1 cup **ORANGE JUICE**

½ teaspoon **CINNAMON**

1 teaspoon alcohol-free **VANILLA**, or 1 teaspoon **VANILLA POWDER**

2 tablespoons **CURRANTS** or unsweetened **DRIED CRANBERRIES**

Place the quinoa, orange juice, cinnamon, and vanilla in a saucepan and bring to a boil. Reduce to a simmer, cover, and cook for 10 to 15 minutes, until all the liquid has been absorbed. Stir in the dried fruit.

Three-Ingredient Waffles

NEW!

3 medium or 2 large very ripe **BANANAS**

1½ cups **ROLLED OATS**

⅓ cup unsweetened **APPLESAUCE**

1 cup **WATER**

Preheat a nonstick waffle iron. Put all the ingredients in a high-powered blender and process until smooth. The batter will be thick. Pour the batter into the waffle iron and cook on high until done, about 10 minutes. Carefully remove the waffle and enjoy!

> **CHEF'S NOTES:** Every waffle iron is different, so there will be a learning curve. These waffles are delicious plain or topped with fruit and drizzled with any California Balsamic brand vinegar. The waffles can be frozen and then reheated or toasted.

Waffle Ice-Cream Sandwiches

NEW!

These are yummy enough to serve as a dessert but healthy enough to have for breakfast.

THREE-INGREDIENT WAFFLES (page 51)

Homemade nondairy **ICE CREAM**

Make your favorite flavor of nondairy ice cream. I simply take ripe bananas, peel and freeze and place them in my Champion juicer. You can also use other machines, such as the Yonanas, a food processor fitted with the "S" blade, or a high-powered blender. If you use a blender, you may have to add a small amount of nondairy milk to get it to process. After the ice cream is made, spread it between 2 waffle squares to make a sandwich and then freeze it. You can roll the edges in low-fat shredded coconut or blueberries.

appeteasers

7

CHAPTER

A Better Bruschetta

This is such a yummy topping, you could even serve it over pasta.

1½ pounds **ROMA TOMATOES**, chopped

1 **RED BELL PEPPER**, chopped

1 (14-ounce) can **ARTICHOKE HEARTS** in water, rinsed, drained, and chopped

1 cup chopped **FRESH BASIL**, packed

½ cup chopped **ITALIAN PARSLEY**, packed

½ cup chopped **RED ONION**

2 tablespoons **BALSAMIC VINEGAR**

3 cloves **GARLIC**, pressed

BAKED TORTILLA CHIPS (page 54)

Put the tomatoes, bell pepper, artichoke hearts, basil, parsley, onion, vinegar, and garlic in a large bowl and mix well. Serve with the tortilla chips.

CHEF'S NOTES: You can certainly chop the vegetables and herbs by hand, or you can put them in a large bowl and use a chopping tool, such as an ulu or mezzaluna, and chop them all together at once. A food processor is not recommended as it will make everything too watery.

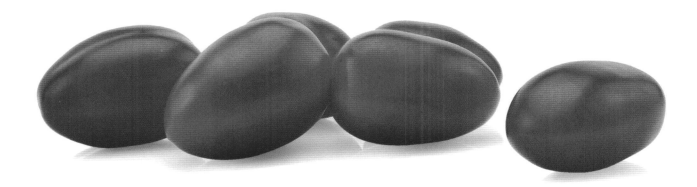

Baked Tortilla Chips

Make sure you get tortillas made with only corn or corn and lime.

Corn **TORTILLAS**

DRIED HERBS or salt-free **SEASONING** blend (optional)

Preheat the oven to 350 degrees F. Line a baking sheet with a nonstick silicone baking mat (such as a Silpat) or with parchment paper.

Cut each tortilla into quarters and arrange them in a single layer on the line baking sheet. Lightly spray each chip with water. Sprinkle with herbs or seasoning blend, if desired. Bake for 10 minutes. Turn the chips over and lightly spray them again with water. Bake for 5 minutes or longer, or until crisp.

> **CHEF'S NOTES:** Silpat mats are very handy. Nothing sticks to them, and they are reusable.

Power Pâté

This tasty appetizer spread is made from peas, onions, and walnuts. The recipe was created by Michelle Wolf, with inspiration from her mother, Pauline. Michelle says it's always a crowd pleaser when her mom serves it to guests.

2 packages frozen **PEAS**, defrosted

2 large Spanish **YELLOW ONIONS**, chopped

1½ cups ground **WALNUTS**

Salt-free **SEASONING** (such as Mrs. Dash or Benson's Table Tasty)

Put the peas in a bowl and mash them with a fork. Alternatively, put them in a food processor and process until smooth. Sauté the onions in water or salt-free vegetable broth. Add to the peas along with the walnuts. Season to taste with salt-free seasoning.

> **CHEF'S NOTES:** This is lovely served on cucumber rounds.

I Can't Believe It's Not Tuna Pâté

Stuff this into endive leaves for a beautiful presentation. It's also delicious on flax crackers, in romaine leaves as a lettuce wrap, or in nori rolls.

1 cup raw **ALMONDS**, soaked in water for 8 to 12 hours

1 cup raw **SUNFLOWER SEEDS**, soaked in water for 8 to 12 hours

Juice from 2 to 3 **LEMONS**

2 stalks **CELERY**, chopped

2 **SCALLIONS**, chopped

½ cup **ITALIAN PARSLEY**, chopped

2 tablespoons **KELP POWDER**

1 tablespoon **DRIED DILL WEED**

1 teaspoon **DULSE POWDER**

Rinse and drain the soaked almonds and sunflower seeds and put them in a food processor fitted with the "S" blade. Add the lemon juice and just enough water to process them into a paste. Transfer to a bowl and stir in the celery, scallions, parsley, kelp powder, dill weed, and dulse powder. Cover and chill in the refrigerator before serving.

> **CHEF'S NOTES:** I like to shape the pâté into a fish with an olive for the eye and serve it over a bed of raw kale.

Caribbean Mango Salsa

Muy sabrosa!

2 (15-ounce) cans salt-free **BLACK BEANS**, rinsed and drained

1 **MANGO**, chopped

1 **CUCUMBER**, peeled, seeded, and chopped

1 **RED BELL PEPPER**, finely chopped

1 bunch **CILANTRO** leaves, chopped

1 bunch **FRESH MINT**, chopped (optional)

1 **AVOCADO**, cubed (optional)

½ small **RED ONION**, finely diced

Zest and juice from 2 **LIMES**

Splash of **ORANGE JUICE**

Pinch of **GROUND CUMIN**

Put all the ingredients in a large bowl and stir until well combined. Chill before serving.

CHEF'S NOTES: If mango is out of season, substitute canned pineapple chunks in their own juice.

Serve in lettuce cups or avocado halves for a spectacular presentation.

Creamy Hummus

A great way to eat more raw veggies.

- 1 (15-ounce) can salt-free **GARBANZO BEANS**
- 2 tablespoons **TAHINI**
- Zest and juice from 1 **LEMON**
- 2 cloves **GARLIC**, plus more to taste
- Pinch of **GROUND CUMIN**

Drain the beans but reserve the liquid. Put the beans, tahini, lemon zest and juice, garlic, and cumin in a food processor fitted with the "S" blade. Process until smooth and creamy, adding as much of the reserved bean liquid as necessary to achieve the desired consistency. Chill before serving.

> **CHEF'S NOTES:** For a lower-fat option, omit the tahini.
>
> You can replace the garbanzo beans with an equal amount of cannellini beans.
>
> Make flavored hummus by adding fresh herbs, such as cilantro, parsley, or scallions. Add roasted red peppers or olives. Substitute roasted garlic for the fresh garlic.

Perfect Pesto-Stuffed Mushrooms

When Rip Esselstyn came to my home for dinner the first time, he ate all twelve stuffed mushrooms by himself!

12 **CREMINI MUSHROOMS**

1 cup **PINE NUTS**

1 cup **FRESH BASIL** leaves, lightly packed

Juice of 1 **LEMON**, plus more as desired

1 tablespoon **YELLOW MISO**

2 cloves **GARLIC**

Remove the stems from the mushrooms. Remove some of the center of the mushrooms if necessary to create a fillable cavity. Put the pine nuts, basil, lemon juice, miso, and garlic in a food processor fitted with the "S" blade and process until smooth. Fill the mushroom caps and dehydrate until warm, 2 to 4 hours. Alternatively, preheat the oven to 350 degrees F. Put the stuffed mushrooms in a baking dish or on a baking sheet and bake for 45 minutes, or until soft.

> **CHEF'S NOTES:** For a lower-fat option, replace the pine nuts with 1 (15-ounce) can garbanzo beans, rinsed and drained.
>
> If you are avoiding all sodium, omit the miso.

Spinach or Kale Dip

I use this dip as the filling for my lasagna.

2 (15-ounce) cans **CANNELLINI BEANS**, rinsed and drained

1 cup **PINE NUTS**, raw **CASHEWS**, or **HEMP SEEDS**

¼ cup **NUTRITIONAL YEAST FLAKES**

¼ cup low-sodium **MISO**

¼ cup freshly squeezed **LEMON JUICE**

2 ounces **FRESH BASIL** leaves

2 cloves **GARLIC**

⅛ teaspoon **RED CHILE FLAKES**

2 pounds frozen chopped **SPINACH** or 1 pound frozen **KALE**, defrosted, drained, and squeezed to remove all the liquid

Put the beans, pine nuts, nutritional yeast, miso, lemon juice, basil, garlic, and chile flakes in a food processor fitted with the "S" blade and process until smooth and creamy. Add the spinach and process until combined.

CHEF'S NOTES: Spoon into a hollowed-out round loaf sourdough bread for a spectacular presentation.

If you are avoiding all sodium, omit the miso. For a lower-fat option, omit the pine nuts.

If you like garlic or red chile flakes, feel free to use more of one or both.

Smokey Chipotle Corn Salsa

This is my all-time favorite salsa.

2 (15-ounce) cans **PINTO BEANS**, drained and rinsed

1 (1-pound) bag frozen **CORN**, defrosted

1 pound **ROMA TOMATOES** (about 4), seeded and diced

1 bunch **CILANTRO**, chopped

4 **SCALLIONS**, finely chopped, plus more as desired

Zest and juice from 4 **LIMES**

1 (4-ounce) can **BLACK OLIVES**, rinsed and drained (optional)

½ teaspoon **CHIPOTLE CHILI POWDER**, or to taste

Put all the ingredients in a large bowl and stir until well combined. Let rest or chill in the refrigerator before serving to allow the flavors to meld. Stir well before serving.

CHEF'S NOTES: This makes a great filling for a burrito. For a lower-fat salsa, omit the olives.

Sweet Pea Guacamole

Much lower in fat and higher in fiber than traditional guacamole.

1 (16-ounce) bag frozen **PEAS**, defrosted

3 firm **ROMA TOMATOES**, diced

1 bunch **CILANTRO**, chopped

1 **JALAPEÑO CHILE**, seeded and finely diced

Juice of 1 **LIME**, or more to taste

1 **SHALLOT**, finely diced

2 cloves **GARLIC**, minced

Pinch **GROUND CUMIN**

Put the peas in a food processor fitted with the "S" blade and process until smooth. Transfer to a large bowl and add the tomatoes, cilantro, chile, lime juice, shallot, garlic, and cumin. Stir until well combined. Cover and chill in the refrigerator before serving.

enticing entrées

8

Mexican Lasagna

This is one of the first recipes I made up when I was a teenager.

4 (15-ounce) cans oil-free low-sodium refried **PINTO BEANS**

2 (16-ounce) bags frozen **CORN**, defrosted

6 cups salt-free **SALSA** or **PICO DE GALLO** (page 124)

2 boxes no-boil brown rice **LASAGNA NOODLES**

Chopped **SCALLIONS** and **OLIVES**, for garnish

Preheat the oven to 350 degrees F. In a large bowl, mix the beans and corn together.

Place 3 cups of the salsa on the bottom of a 9 x 13-inch pan. Place one-third of the noodles over the salsa, and spoon half of the bean and corn mixture over the noodles. Place another third of the noodles on the corn and bean mixture, then top with the remaining corn and bean mixture. Place the remaining noodles on top of the corn and bean mixture and the remaining 3 cups of salsa over the top layer of noodles. Make sure the top layer of noodles is completely covered with salsa.

Bake uncovered for 30 minutes or until heated through. Let sit for 10 minutes before slicing. Garnish with chopped scallions and olives, if desired.

CHEF'S NOTES: This is great with a dollop of Sweet Pea Guacamole (page 61) on top.

Canned refried beans do not come without salt. To make this recipe completely salt-free, mash 4 (15-ounce) cans salt-free pinto beans.

You can also use lasagna noodles made from hearts of palm, available online and at many natural food stores.

Chef AJ's Disappearing Lasagna

People always ask me how well this freezes. I honestly don't know as there have never been any leftovers!

6 cups oil-free MARINARA SAUCE

2 (15-ounce) cans CANNELLINI BEANS, rinsed and drained

1 cup PINE NUTS, raw CASHEWS, or HEMP SEEDS

¼ cup NUTRITIONAL YEAST FLAKES

¼ cup low-sodium MISO

¼ cup freshly squeezed LEMON JUICE

2 ounces FRESH BASIL leaves

⅛ teaspoon RED CHILE FLAKES, plus more as desired

2 pounds frozen chopped SPINACH or 1 pound frozen KALE, defrosted, drained, and squeezed to remove all the liquid

1 large RED ONION, minced

2 pounds sliced CREMINI or BABY BELLA MUSHROOMS

¼ cup low-sodium TAMARI

2 cloves GARLIC, plus more as desired

1 (4-ounce) can sliced OLIVES, drained and rinsed (optional)

FAUX PARMESAN (page 127)

2 boxes no-boil brown rice LASAGNA NOODLES

Preheat the oven to 375 degrees F.

To make the filling, put the beans, pine nuts, nutritional yeast, miso, lemon juice, basil, garlic, and chile flakes in a food processor fitted with the "S" blade and process until smooth. Add the spinach or kale and process until well incorporated.

In a large nonstick sauté pan, sauté the onion in 2 tablespoons of water until translucent, about 8 minutes, adding more water, 1 tablespoon at a time, if necessary to prevent sticking. Add the mushrooms, tamari, and garlic and sauté until the mushrooms are browned. Taste and add more garlic or tamari as desired. Cook until the mushrooms look glazed and there is no more liquid left in the pan.

To assemble the lasagna, pour 3 cups of the marinara sauce into a lasagna pan or 9 x 13-inch pan. Place one layer of the noodles on top of the sauce. Cover the noodles with half of the bean mixture, then cover the bean mixture with half of the mushroom mixture. Place another layer of noodles over the mushroom mixture and top with the remaining bean mixture followed by the remaining mushroom mixture. Place one more layer of noodles on top of the mushroom mixture and evenly cover with the remaining marinara sauce. Sprinkle the olives over the top and dust liberally with Faux Parmesan.

Bake uncovered for 1 hour. Let rest for 10 minutes before slicing and serving.

CHEF'S NOTES: If you have time, marinate the sliced mushrooms in the tamari several hours in advance or even the night before.

Make sure the top layer of noodles is fully covered with sauce.

If you are avoiding all sodium, omit the miso and use California Balsamic Gilroy Garlic vinegar in place of the tamari.

You can also use lasagna noodles made from hearts of palm. These are available online and at many natural food stores.

Hearty Lentil Loaf

No soy or bread crumbs in this loaf, just whole-food goodness.

3 cups cooked **LENTILS**

1 (16-ounce) bag frozen **CARROTS**, defrosted and drained

2 cups chopped **RED ONION** (about 1 large)

2 cloves **GARLIC**, peeled

½ cup chopped **ITALIAN PARSLEY**, finely chopped

2 cups raw **WALNUTS**, divided

2 cups uncooked **OATS** (not instant), divided

Salt-free **SEASONING**

Preheat the oven to 350 degrees F.

Combine the lentils, carrots, onion, garlic, parsley, one cup of the walnuts, and one cup of the oats in a food processor fitted with the "S" blade. Process the ingredients until smooth and almost paste-like. Place the mixture in a bowl and stir in the remaining oats, chopped walnuts, and seasoning, to taste.

Pour the mixture into a standard silicone loaf pan, and bake uncovered for 50 to 55 minutes, until golden brown. Remove from the oven and let sit for at least 10 minutes, invert onto a serving dish; let cool for another 5 minutes and slice.

CHEF'S NOTES: I also like to make this in a silicone Bundt pan and fill it with 5-Minute Cranberry Relish (page 122).

For a reduced-fat version, substitute 2 cups chopped mushrooms for the walnuts. May need seasoning.

You can use a 19-ounce box of Trader Joe's cooked lentils to save time.

This is delicious even without any sauce or gravy of any kind, or add your favorite condiments such as ketchup, mustard, or BBQ Sauce.

Stuff cold leftovers into pita pockets for a great lunch!

Lentil Tacos

One of my students, Karen Spector, brought this to a potluck, and it was a huge hit. Karen won an award where she worked for being the "green smoothie queen."

1 cup chopped **ONION**

1 **GARLIC** clove, minced

1 cup dry **LENTILS**, rinsed

1 tablespoon **CHILI POWDER**

2 teaspoons **GROUND CUMIN**

1 teaspoon **OREGANO**

14 ounces **WATER**

1 cup salt-free **SALSA** or **PICO DE GALLO** (page 124)

Salt-free **SEASONING**, to taste

Combine all the ingredients in a crock pot, and cook on high for 8 to 12 hours, stirring occasionally and adding water as needed.

CHEF'S NOTES: This taco filling can be used anywhere you would normally use a meat taco filling, such as in taco shells and on salads.

You can buy a slow cooker now for under 20 bucks. It is a great investment and I guarantee you will use it. You can put up a quick soup or stew in the morning and have a hot, healthy dinner ready for you when you come home.

Melanzana Abbodanza

Which translated means "eggplant abundance."

1 recipe **CHEF AJ'S DISAPPEARING LASAGNA** (page 64), minus the rice lasagna noodles

2 large **EGGPLANTS**

Salt-free **SEASONING**, to taste

Preheat the oven to 400 degrees F.

Slice the unpeeled eggplant into ¼ inch thick and place on a Silpat baking mat or a nonstick baking sheet pan. Sprinkle with your favorite salt-free seasoning.

Bake for 20 minutes. Turn the slices over and bake for an additional 20 minutes, or until the eggplant begins to shrink and soften.

Follow the directions for the lasagna but use the baked eggplant slices in place of the noodles.

> **CHEF'S NOTES:** You can substitute thinly sliced zucchini for the eggplant.

Not So Sloppy Joes

This is great served over a bed of steamed kale.

2 cups diced **RED ONION**

2 cups diced **RED BELL PEPPER**

2 cloves **GARLIC**, pressed

1 (14.5 ounce) can diced salt-free **TOMATOES**

1 (6 ounce) **can salt-free TOMATO PASTE**

1 teaspoon **CHILI POWDER**

2 (15-ounce) **cans salt-free BLACK BEANS**, drained

1 **LIME**, juiced

Dry sauté the onions, peppers, and garlic in a hot nonstick pan over high heat for 7 to 8 minutes, until soft and translucent. Add the diced tomatoes, tomato paste, chili powder, and beans. Stir until well combined and cook for another 2 to 3 minutes, until heated. Remove from the heat and stir in the lime juice.

Smoky Sweet Potato Burgers   *NEW!*

Many plant-based burger recipes, while delicious, have a long list of ingredients and lots of preparation steps. This one contains five common, easy-to-find ingredients, as well as a few spices that you may already have on hand. (For the best flavor, be sure the paprika you use is smoked—not regular or hot.)

1 (16-ounce) **bag frozen BROCCOLI**

4 cups cooked **ORANGE SWEET POTATO**, peeled and mashed

1 cup chopped **GREEN SCALLIONS**

2 cups cooked **RICE** (I like to use white basmati or whatever I have leftover)

2 cups **ROLLED OATS**

2 tablespoons **SMOKED PAPRIKA**

1 teaspoon **ONION POWDER**

1 teaspoon **GARLIC POWDER**

1 teaspoon **CHIPOTLE POWDER**

Preheat the oven to 400 degrees F.

Steam or boil the broccoli according to your preferred preparation method. I simply microwave it with a bit of water in a microwave steamer for 5 minutes, until very soft. Drain and mash with a fork.

Combine all the remaining ingredients with the broccoli and mix well until fully incorporated. Measure out about ½ cup of the mixture and flatten into a burger. Place on a Silpat or other nonstick silicone baking mat or piece of parchment paper. Bake for 30 to 45 minutes, or until you can turn them over easily without them falling apart. Carefully flip the burgers with a spatula and cook for another 10 to 15 minutes.

CHEF'S NOTES: These burgers freeze very well, and you can simply heat them up in the microwave or air fryer.

You can serve them on potato waffle buns, in lettuce or collard wraps, or open face on purple cabbage leaves. You can use any condiments you like, but they are especially good with Zesty Mango Salsa (page 123) or even a swipe of Ultimate Sauce (page 95).

Cook the sweet potatoes according to your preferred method. I find they are tastier when roasted at 400 degrees F for about an hour, or until soft. Peel the potatoes while still warm and refrigerate overnight.

Smoky BBQ Sweet Potato Loaf   *NEW!*

If you don't have time to bake this as a loaf, you can make the batter into burgers or in a muffin tin to decrease the cooking time by half an hour. This is even better the next day, after it has time to firm up, and it also freezes very well. (For the best flavor, be sure the paprika you use is smoked—not regular or hot.)

1 (16-ounce) **bag frozen BROCCOLI**

4 cups cooked **ORANGE SWEET POTATO**, peeled and mashed

1 cup chopped **GREEN SCALLIONS**

2 cups **ROLLED OATS**

2 cups cooked **RICE** (I like to use white Basmati or whatever I have leftover)

2 tablespoons **SMOKED PAPRIKA**

1 teaspoon **ONION POWDER**

1 teaspoon **GARLIC POWDER**

¾ teaspoon **CHIPOTLE POWDER**

EASY BBQ SAUCE (page 94)

Preheat the oven to 400 degrees F.

Steam or boil the broccoli according to your preferred preparation method. I simply microwave it with a bit or water in a Pampered Chef microwave steamer for 5 minutes until very soft. Then drain and mash with a fork.

Combine all the remaining ingredients to the broccoli and mix well until fully incorporated. Evenly pour the batter into a silicone loaf pan, cover with BBQ sauce, and bake for 75 minutes. Remove from the oven and let sit at least 15 minutes before slicing.

> **CHEF'S NOTES:** For an adorable presentation, bake in silicone muffin tins and decrease baking time to 45 minutes.
>
> Cook the sweet potatoes according to your preferred method. I find they are tastier when roasted at 400 degrees F for about an hour, or until soft. Peel the potatoes while still warm and refrigerate overnight.

Over-The-Rainbow Lettuce Cups
with Sweet Potato Croutons *NEW!*

Lettuce leaves make perfect containers or "cups" for this delicious filling.

1 large **SWEET ONION**, chopped

8 **GARLIC** cloves, peeled and finely chopped

1 pound **RAINBOW CHARD**, chopped

3 cups cooked **RICE** or other cooked grain of your choice (quinoa, millet etc.)

LETTUCE leaves of choice for cups (Boston, Bibb, Romaine)

ULTIMATE SAUCE (page 95)

CROUTONS, to top

Dry sauté the onions in a hot pan over high heat until caramelized, adding water a tablespoon at a time if necessary to keep it from sticking. When the onions are as brown as you like, add the chopped garlic and sauté a minute or two longer.

Turn the heat to medium and add the chopped chard, cooking until soft and bright green. This will not take very long, maybe a minute or two.

Fill the lettuce leaves with the cooked rice, then the greens mixture and the Ultimate Sauce. Alternatively, you can mix the sauce into the greens. Top with the croutons.

> **CHEF'S NOTES:** If you do not want to use Ultimate Sauce, stir into the greens while cooking a 14.5–ounce can of Muir Glen salt-free fire roasted tomatoes and 1 tablespoon Italian seasoning. Then drizzle the lettuce cups with your favorite reduced balsamic vinegar. I like brands that are flavored with hickory smoke.
>
> This is a great recipe for using frozen rice or other grains.

Sweet Potato Croutons

These crunchy little gems can also be used on salads to make them even more special.

SWEET POTATOES

Preheat the oven to 400 degrees F.

Cut the sweet potatoes into small cubes, no more than ¼ inch. Place on a nonstick silicone baking sheet or a piece of parchment paper, and bake for 25 to 30 minutes, until the edges of the cubes are golden brown but not burned.

> **CHEF'S NOTES:** To save time, substitute bags of frozen cubed sweet potatoes, butternut squash or Kabocha squash for the uncooked sweet potatoes.
>
> You can bake the cubes in an air fryer at 400 degrees F for about 20 minutes.

Sweet and Sour Tempeh

1 pound **TEMPEH**

1½ cups unsweetened **PINEAPPLE JUICE**

½ cup unsweetened **KETCHUP**

½ cup **DATE SYRUP**

¼ cup unsweetened **RICE VINEGAR**

3 tablespoons **ARROWROOT POWDER**

1 clove **GARLIC** (or more to taste)

1 inch piece **FRESH GINGER** (or more to taste)

1 **GREEN BELL PEPPER**, cut into squares

Cut the tempeh into triangles. Combine all ingredients in a saucepan except for the tempeh and green pepper. Heat and stir until boiling. Reduce the heat and simmer until thickened. Keep warm.

Add the tempeh to a hot wok or nonstick skillet, and sauté in a little water until browned. Add the sauce and green pepper and cook briefly until hot.

Portobello Mushroom Stroganoff

SAUCE

1 (12.4 ounce) box Mori Nu SILKEN TOFU

½ cup WATER

3 tablespoons fresh LEMON JUICE

Zest from one LEMON

3 tablespoons low-sodium TAMARI

2 tablespoons TAHINI

2 cloves GARLIC

1-inch piece FRESH GINGER, or to taste

FILLING

1 RED ONION, minced

1 pound PORTOBELLO MUSHROOMS, sliced

1 teaspoon OREGANO

Chopped ITALIAN PARSLEY, for garnish

Place all ingredients for the sauce in a blender, and process until smooth.

Dry sauté the onions in a hot nonstick pan over high heat until translucent. Add the mushrooms and sauté until they become limp and the moisture they exude has evaporated. Stir in the oregano. Pour the sauce over the vegetables and mix well. Garnish with fresh parsley.

CHEF'S NOTES: This is great served over brown rice.

For a lower-fat option, substitute one (15-ounce) can cannellini beans for the tofu and tahini.

Quick Sun-Dried Tomato Marinara

This sauce takes minutes to make but tastes like it was slow simmered for hours. The best part is, there are no pots to clean or vegetables to cut up.

1 cup oil-free **SUN-DRIED TOMATOES**, soaked in water

3 or 4 fresh **ROMA TOMATOES**

1 **RED BELL PEPPER**, seeded

1 or 2 cloves **GARLIC**, peeled

3 or 4 pitted **DATES**

1 **SHALLOT**, or 1 tablespoon chopped **RED ONION**

3 or 4 **FRESH BASIL** leaves

In a blender, process all the ingredients until smooth. If you prefer a chunkier consistency, use a food processor fitted with the "S" blade and process all the ingredients until the desired consistency is reached.

Serve over your favorite healthy noodles, such as those made from rice, tofu, sea vegetables, hearts of palm, legumes, sweet potatoes, or zucchini. To make zucchini noodles, peel the zucchini and cut into noodles using a spiralizer or vegetable peeler.

> **CHEF'S NOTES:** If you have a high-powered blender, you can make this sauce hot right in the blender.

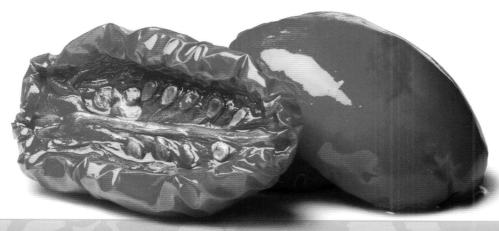

Stirred, Not Fried

I like to use broccoli, bok choy, pea pods, carrots, peas, corn, red bell pepper, red onion, bean sprouts, and cilantro.

1 cup raw **ALMOND BUTTER**

1 ripe **AVOCADO**

Zest and juice from 3 **LIMES** (about ⅓ cup juice)

3 tablespoons low-sodium **TAMARI**

4 to 6 cloves **GARLIC**

1-inch piece **FRESH GINGER**, peeled

1 teaspoon **TAMARIND PASTE**

6 **DATES**

10 to 20 **MINT** leaves

RED PEPPER FLAKES (optional)

½ cup **WATER** (or water from a Thai young coconut)

Chopped **ALMONDS**, **BEAN SPROUTS**, and chopped **CILANTRO**, for garnish

Your favorite **RAW VEGGIES**, cut up in small pieces

To make the sauce, place all the ingredients except the raw veggies in a blender and process until smooth, adding only enough water to allow the ingredients to move easily. Pour over the vegetables and coat well. Top with bean sprouts, chopped almonds, and cilantro, if desired.

CHEF'S NOTES: This dish is even better the next day, after the flavors have a chance to marinate.

For a reduced-fat version, substitute chestnuts for the almond butter and the avocado, or substitute salt-free, sugar-free powdered almond butter for the raw almond butter.

For a no-sodium option, substitute California Balsamic Teriyaki vinegar for the tamari.

Stuffed Butternut Squash

This has been my favorite fall entrée since I was seven years old.

3 or 4 BUTTERNUT SQUASHES (depending on their size)

4 cups GRAIN of choice (brown rice, quinoa)

1 RED ONION, chopped

2 cups chopped CELERY

2 cups chopped MUSHROOMS

1 cup chopped FRESH ITALIAN PARSLEY

KATHY HESTER SAUSAGE CRUMBLES (page 80)

Preheat the oven to 400 degrees F.

Cut the squash in half and bake, cut side down, on a Silpat mat or nonstick pan approximately 40 minutes, until soft. Remove the seeds. Scoop out the squash, leaving a wall ¼-inch thick, and place in a large bowl.

Prepare your grain of choice according to package directions and set aside.

In a large pan, sauté the onion, celery, and mushrooms in a tablespoon of water until soft, about 10 minutes. Add the Sausage Crumbles and sauté until browned. Add the vegetables, Crumbles, and parsley to the squash and mix well. Add the grain to the squash mixture.

Fill the squash halves with the stuffing mixture. Bake for another 30 minutes, until browned.

> **CHEF'S NOTES:** Sometimes I add dried unsweetened cranberries and pecans to the stuffing.

Sweet Potato Nachos

When you're vegan, not many people invite you over for dinner. And when you are a chef, even fewer do! My friend Margaret Rudoy dared to have me over and created this delicious dish that is now a staple in our home and appears in the beautiful cover photo of this new edition.

SWEET POTATOES (one per person)

SMOKED PAPRIKA

Your favorite **NACHO TOPPINGS** (such as oil-free refried beans, chopped tomato, corn, cilantro, onion, olives, jalapeño chiles)

Preheat the oven to 450 degrees F.

Cut the sweet potato into uniform slices, approximately ¼ inch thick. Place on a Silpat mat or nonstick baking sheet, and sprinkle with smoked paprika. Bake for 20 minutes, turn over, and bake for another 10 to 15 minutes, until crisp. These are the "chips" for your nachos.

To serve, place several sweet potato "chips" on a plate, and fully load them with your favorite nacho toppings.

> **CHEF'S NOTES:** I like to create a nacho bar so guests can build their own nachos.
>
> If you use organic sweet potatoes, there is no need to peel them. The skins contain lots of fiber and other nutrients.

Kathy Hester Sausage Crumbles

Thank you, Kathy, for the wonderful recipe!

1 cup **WATER**

½ cup steel-cut gluten-free **OATS**

2 teaspoon rubbed **SAGE**

2 teaspoon **MARJORAM**

1½ teaspoon granulated **GARLIC**

1 teaspoon **BASIL**

1 teaspoon **FENNEL SEEDS**

1 teaspoon **THYME**

1 teaspoon **OREGANO**

¼ teaspoon **CAYENNE**, or to taste

¼ to ⅛ teaspoon **BLACK PEPPER**

¼ teaspoon **GROUND ROSEMARY**

Preheat the oven to 350 degrees F and cover a baking sheet with parchment paper.

In a saucepan, add the water and oats, bring to a boil, then turn the heat to low and cover. Cook for 10 minutes. Mix the remaining ingredients in a bowl and set aside.

Remove the cover from the oats for 5 minutes and stir occasionally to reduce any liquid in the bottom of the pan. Remove from the heat, add the combined herbs and spices, and mix well.

Spoon the oat mixture onto the parchment paper, spreading it out over the sheet. Place a second piece of parchment paper on top and flatten the mixture as much as possible.

Bake for 10 minutes, then remove from the oven and cut lines into the oat mixture with a knife to allow the steam to escape.

Bake for 5 more minutes. Remove from the oven, scraping up the Sausage with a spatula and breaking it up into crumbles. Return to the oven and bake 5 for more minutes, then remove and crumble one more time. Allow to cool before using.

CHEF'S NOTES: You can sprinkle Sausage Crumbles on pizza and even freeze leftovers for later!

Sweet Potato and Blue Corn Enchiladas

ENCHILADA SAUCE

1 **RED ONION**, chopped

2 cloves **GARLIC**, crushed

1½ cups **WATER**

1 (28-ounce) **can** salt-free **TOMATOES**

3 tablespoons **CHILI POWDER**

1 teaspoon **CUMIN**

1 tablespoon low-sodium **TAMARI**

3 tablespoons **ARROWROOT POWDER**

Sliced **OLIVES** and chopped **SCALLIONS** (optional)
SWEET PEA GUACAMOLE (page 61)

FILLING

3 cups mashed cooked **SWEET POTATOES**

2 cups **PICO DE GALLO** (page 124) or salt-free **SALSA**

1-pound bag frozen roasted **CORN**, defrosted

12 blue corn **TORTILLAS**

To prepare the sauce, place the onion, garlic, and water in a pot, and cook for 8 to 10 minutes, until soft. Stir in the tomatoes, chili powder, and cumin, and cook on low heat for 15 minutes. Add the tamari and arrowroot powder and stir until thickened.

Prepare the filling by combining the sweet potatoes, salsa, and roasted corn. Preheat the oven to 350 degrees F.

Cover the bottom of a baking dish with half the Enchilada Sauce. Spread the filling down the center of each tortilla. Roll up and place seam side down in the dish. Pour the remaining sauce over the tortillas and sprinkle with sliced olives, if using. Bake for 30 minutes. Sprinkle with chopped scallions and top with Sweet Pea Guacamole if desired.

> **CHEF'S NOTES:** For a low-sodium option, substitute California Balsamic Gilroy Garlic vinegar for the tamari.

salads, dressings, & sauces

Hail to the Kale Salad

Even people who say they don't like kale will gobble this up. Like a woman, this only gets better with age, so it's a great dish to make ahead of time.

DRESSING

1 cup unsweetened, unsalted raw **ALMOND BUTTER**

1 cup **COCONUT WATER** or plain water

¼ cup fresh **LIME JUICE**

2 cloves **GARLIC**

Fresh, peeled **FRESH GINGER** (approximately 1 inch or ½ ounce)

2 tablespoons low-sodium **TAMARI**

4 pitted **DATES**, soaked in water if not soft

½ teaspoon **RED CHILE FLAKES**

24 ounces **KALE** (about two bunches)

SEEDS or chopped **NUTS**

In a high-powered blender, combine all the dressing ingredients and process until smooth and creamy. Remove the large, thick stems from the kale. Finely chop the kale leaves and place in a large bowl. Pour 2 cups of the dressing over the kale and massage the dressing into the kale with your fingers. Sprinkle with seeds or nuts before serving, if desired. Refrigerate any unused dressing.

CHEF'S NOTES: You can make a low-fat, low-sodium option by using 2 cups roasted chestnuts instead of almond butter and 2 tablespoons California Balsamic Teriyaki or Gilroy Garlic vinegar instead of the tamari. Use 8 dates instead of 4. One cup of almond butter has 1,600 calories and 148 grams of fat; in comparison, one cup of chestnuts has only 320 calories and 4 grams of fat.

For another low-fat option, substitute 1 (15-ounce) can cannellini beans (rinsed and drained) plus 6 tablespoons almond butter for the 1 cup almond butter.

If you have an ulu knife (a rocking blade with a wooden handle), you can use it to chop the kale leaves directly in a wooden salad bowl and massage in the dressing at the same time.

Nostada Salad

We served this at the Challenge dinners to show people how you can make a hot, healthy, delicious meal in no time. When they tasted it, they began to realize that you don't need oil to enjoy a delicious salad.

ROMAINE LETTUCE, chopped

Frozen **CORN**, warmed

Oil-free **REFRIED BEANS**, warmed

Chopped **TOMATOES**

Chopped **SCALLIONS**

Chopped **CILANTRO**

OLIVES and **PUMPKIN SEEDS**, for garnish

Fresh **LIME JUICE**

Place the lettuce in a large bowl. Add a big scoop of warmed corn and beans. Top with the tomatoes, scallions, cilantro, and top with olives and pumpkin seeds, if desired. Squeeze lime juice over the top and enjoy immediately.

CHEF'S NOTES: Also good on this is Pico de Gallo (page 124) and Sweet Pea Guacamole (page 61).

Cucumber-Peanut Salad

3 large **CUCUMBERS**, peeled, seeded, and chopped (about 2 pounds)

Zest and juice from 2 **LIMES**

RED PEPPER FLAKES, to taste

Chopped **FRESH MINT**

½ cup chopped roasted unsalted **PEANUTS**

Mix all ingredients except for the peanuts and combine well. Let flavors meld at least 30 minutes before serving. Add the chopped peanuts right before serving.

CHEF'S NOTES: You can substitute fresh basil or cilantro for the mint.

For a lower-fat option, omit the peanuts.

Fennel Salad

One of my Kitchen Angels, Ellen Greek, brought this to a potluck. Hard to believe that something with only three ingredients could be so delicious.

2 bulbs **FENNEL**

20 **DATES**

LEMON JUICE, to taste

Slice the fennel bulb very thinly and place in a bowl. Set aside the green top in one piece to decorate the salad. Slice the dates and mix them with the fennel slices. Pour the lemon juice over and mix all the ingredients well.

CHEF'S NOTES: You can serve this cold or at room temperature.

If using fresh lemons, add the zest.

Spinach Waldorf

I served this beautiful dish to Chef Brian Malarkey on *Kick-Off Cookoff*.

1 recipe **HAIL TO THE KALE SALAD DRESSING** (page 83)

SPINACH

Thinly sliced **RED APPLES**

Shredded **CARROTS**

Shredded **BEETS**

Chopped **WALNUTS**

POMEGRANATE SEEDS

Place the spinach, apples, carrots, and beets in a large bowl and toss with Hail to the Kale dressing. Sprinkle the walnuts and pomegranate seeds on top before serving.

CHEF'S NOTES: For a lower-fat dressing, use a reduced-fat option given in the chef's notes of the Hail to the Kale recipe, page 83.

Ginger Slaw

SLAW

2 cups shredded **CARROTS**

2 cups shredded **PURPLE CABBAGE**

2 cups **JICAMA**, cut into long thin strips

CILANTRO and **PUMPKIN SEEDS**, for garnish

DRESSING

½ cup **ORANGE JUICE**

Zest and juice from one **LIME**

½ ounce **FRESH GINGER**, pressed (2 tablespoons, sliced)

CILANTRO and **PUMPKIN SEEDS**, for garnish

Combine the vegetables for the slaw in a large bowl. Whisk together the dressing ingredients and pour over the vegetables. Garnish with cilantro and pumpkin seeds if desired.

Artichoke and Sun-Dried Tomato Pasta Salad

NEW!

All of your favorite pizza toppings make a terrific salad.

1 pound **PASTA** (your favorite), **cooked and chilled**

1 (14-ounce) **bag frozen ARTICHOKES,** defrosted

1 (3-ounce) **bag oil-free SUN-DRIED TOMATOES** (about ¾ cup)

1 cup chopped **FRESH BASIL** (about ¾ ounce)

1 cup roasted **GARLIC** cloves

½ cup California Balsamic 7-Herb **ITALIAN VINEGAR** (or your favorite oil-free Italian salad dressing)

Combine all the ingredients in a large bowl and enjoy!

CHEF'S NOTES: Black olives also make an excellent addition to this salad.

To easily roast garlic, place in an air fryer at 370 degrees F for 10 minutes.

Easy Four-Bean Salad

NEW!

The perfect dish for picnics, parties, and potlucks, I promise you that no one will miss that it's not swimming in oil.

1 (15-ounce) **can GARBANZO BEANS** (or 1½ cups cooked beans)

1 (15-ounce) **can KIDNEY BEANS** (or 1½ cups cooked beans)

1 (15-ounce) **can WHITE BEANS** (or 1½ cups cooked beans)

8 ounces cut **GREEN BEANS** (defrost if using frozen)

½ **RED ONION,** finely chopped (about 1 cup), **to taste**

½ cup California Balsamic 7-Herb **ITALIAN VINEGAR** (or to taste) **or** your favorite oil-free Italian salad dressing.

Chopped **PARSLEY,** for garnish

Rinse and drain the beans. Mix all the ingredients together in a large bowl. Stir in the vinegar, combine well, and chill. Garnish with fresh chopped parsley, if desired.

Artichoke-Brazil Nut Dressing

This recipe was inspired by Zel Allen, author of *The Nut Gourmet* and publisher of vegparadise.com.

½ cup raw **BRAZIL NUTS**

1 (14-ounce) **can water-packed ARTICHOKE HEARTS**, rinsed and drained

1 cup unsweetened **ALMOND MILK**

¼ cup fresh **LEMON JUICE**

¼ cup **RICE VINEGAR**

¼ cup **NUTRITIONAL YEAST FLAKES**

1 teaspoon salt-free **SEASONING** (or to taste)

Grind the Brazil nuts in a blender or in a coffee grinder. Place the remaining ingredients in the blender along with the nuts, and process until smooth and creamy.

> **CHEF'S NOTES:** Nutritional yeast, high in B vitamins, is different than brewer's yeast. It is often found in the bulk section or supplement section of natural food stores.

Cara Cara Balsamic Dressing   *NEW!*

If you can't find Cara Cara oranges, feel free to use any orange that tastes sweet.

1 (12-ounce) bag **RICED CAULIFLOWER**

1 cup fresh squeezed **CARA CARA ORANGE JUICE**

½ cup reduced **BALSAMIC VINEGAR** (4% acidity preferred)

2 tablespoons stone-ground **MUSTARD** (I use Westbrae salt-free)

2 large cloves **GARLIC**

1 tablespoon **CHIA SEEDS**

Steam the cauliflower in ½ cup of water. (I use the Pampered Chef microwave steamer for 6 minutes.) Chill the cauliflower and its cooking liquid.

Place the chilled cauliflower and liquid in a high-powered blender with the remaining ingredients, and process until smooth and creamy. Store in the refrigerator.

> **CHEF'S NOTES:** Cara Cara oranges tend to be sweeter and less acidic than regular juice oranges. Sometimes commercial orange juice can taste bitter.

Aunt Melony's Caesar Salad Dressing

Melony Jorenson was a past winner of the "Unprocessed Challenge." She created this delicious, creamy nut-free dressing.

1 cup **WATER**

1 (15-ounce) can **CANNELLINI BEANS**, drained and rinsed

3 cloves **GARLIC**

¾ cup **LEMON JUICE**

4 tablespoons low-sodium **MISO**

6 tablespoons **NUTRITIONAL YEAST FLAKES**

1 tablespoon **RICE VINEGAR**

1 tablespoon salt-free **MUSTARD**

1 teaspoon **ONION POWDER**

1 tablespoon **CHIA SEEDS**

Place all the ingredients except the chia seeds in a blender and process until smooth. Add the chia seeds and blend again briefly.

> **CHEF'S NOTES:** This dressing is delicious on baked potatoes and steamed veggies.
>
> If you are avoiding all sodium, omit the miso.

Creamy Seven-Herb Italian Dressing   *NEW!*

This makes a delicious creamy salad dressing, dip, or spread.

1 (12-ounce bag) **CAULIFLOWER florets** (about 4 cups)

¼ cup California Balsamic 7-Herb **ITALIAN VINEGAR**

Steam the cauliflower according to the package directions, then chill. Place the steamed cauliflower and vinegar in a high-powered blender, and puree until smooth and creamy. Store in the refrigerator.

Green Goodness Dressing

If you use only the tops of the scallions, the dressing will be really bright green like Green Goddess.

2 cups filtered WATER

1 cup fresh LEMON JUICE

⅔ cup SESAME SEEDS

⅓ cup low-sodium MISO

2 cloves GARLIC

½ ounce FRESH GINGER

8 deglet noor DATES, or to taste

½ bunch SCALLIONS (about 3 ounces)

1 tablespoon CHIA SEEDS

Place all ingredients except for the chia seeds in a high-powered blender, and process until smooth. Adjust the flavors to taste. Add the chia seeds and blend again briefly. Store in the refrigerator.

> **CHEF'S NOTES:** If you are avoiding all sodium, omit the miso.

Hemp Seed-Lime Dressing

½ cup HEMP SEEDS

Zest from 1 LIME

½ cup LIME JUICE

1½ cups WATER

1 (1-inch) piece FRESH GINGER, or

more to taste

2 cloves GARLIC, or more to taste

4 whole pitted DATES, or more to taste

1 tablespoon salt-free SEASONING

1 tablespoon CHIA SEEDS

Place all the ingredients except the chia seeds in a high-powered blender, and process until smooth and creamy. Adjust the flavors to taste. Add the chia seeds and blend again briefly.

> **CHEF'S NOTES:** If you can't find hemp seeds, substitute soaked cashews.

Creamy Roasted Garlic Balsamic Dressing   *NEW!*

¼ cup roasted peeled **GARLIC** cloves

1 (12-ounce bag) **CAULIFLOWER** florets

½ cup **BALSAMIC VINEGAR** (a good-quality reduced brand that is 4% acidity is preferred)

½ cup **WATER**

2 tablespoons stone ground **MUSTARD** (I prefer Westbrae salt-free)

1 to 2 tablespoons **ITALIAN SEASONING** (optional)

Roast the peeled garlic cloves according to your preferred method. I like to air fry them at 370 degrees F for 10 minutes.

Cook the cauliflower using the method you prefer. (I use the Pampered Chef microwave steamer for 6 minutes with a bit of water.) Drain and chill.

Place the chilled cooked cauliflower in a high-powered blender with the remaining ingredients, and blend until smooth. Store in the refrigerator

CHEF'S NOTES: I love the organic, non-irradiated spices from LocalSpicery. com. You can get two free small samples using the code: CHEF AJ.

Orange-Sesame Dressing

I made this up during a class to show how easy it is to "just throw stuff in a blender" and make a delicious dressing.

3 or 4 peeled **ORANGES**

½ cup **SESAME SEEDS**

2 tablespoons low-sodium **MISO**

Place all ingredients in a high-powered blender, and process until smooth.

CHEF'S NOTES: This is especially delicious on chopped kale.

If you are avoiding all sodium, omit the miso.

Creamy Southwestern Ranch Dressing   *NEW!*

This dressing will make you fall in love with your salads again. Slightly sweet, slightly smoky with just a little bit of heat.

- 1 (12-ounce bag) **CAULIFLOWER**, steamed and chilled
- 4 ounces pitted **DATES**
- ½ cup **LIME JUICE**
- 1 cup **WATER**
- 2 teaspoons **SMOKED PAPRIKA** (must be smoked, not sweet)
- ¼ teaspoon **CHIPOTLE POWDER**

Place all the ingredients in a high-powered blender, and process until smooth and creamy. Store in the refrigerator.

> **CHEF'S NOTES:** Most vegan recipes use tofu, nuts, or beans for creaminess. Those are certainly healthy options, but I much prefer to use vegetables.
>
> This is also delicious on sweet corn on the cob and over rice and beans.
>
> It's a great way to sneak in extra vegetables, and you don't have to worry about portion control because the entire batch has fewer calories than 3 tablespoons of olive oil.

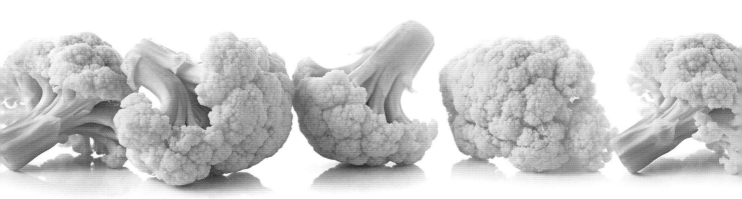

Hummus Dressing

1 cup **CREAMY HUMMUS** (page 57)

3 tablespoons fresh **LEMON JUICE**

3 tablespoons fresh **LIME JUICE**

3 tablespoons **ORANGE JUICE**

1 tablespoon salt-free stone-ground **MUSTARD**

3 soft pitted **DATES**

1 clove **GARLIC**, or more to taste

1 (½-inch) piece **FRESH GINGER**, or more to taste

½ cup raw **CASHEWS**

Place all the ingredients except the cashews in a high-powered blender, and process until smooth. Add the cashews and blend again until thick and creamy. Store in the refrigerator

CHEF'S NOTES: For a lower-fat option, omit the cashews.

Easy BBQ Sauce

Most barbecue sauces are very high in sugar. Here the sweetness comes just from the grapes in the vinegar.

2 tablespoon **TOMATO PASTE**

2 tablespoons California Balsamic Smoked **HICKORY VINEGAR**, or more, to taste

Combine both ingredients and store in the refrigerator.

CHEF'S NOTES: I always have tomato paste and this balsamic vinegar on hand to make a quick dip for my air fries in no time.

Ultimate Sauce

This is the *ultimate* in sauces!

1 (15-ounce) **can salt-free GARBANZO BEANS, rinsed and drained** (or 1½ cups cooked beans)

1 cup **WATER**

2 ounces pitted **DATES** (approximately 8 deglet noor or 4 medjool dates)

Zest of 1 **LIME** (optional)

4 tablespoons of **LIME JUICE**

1 tablespoon unsweetened, unseasoned **RICE VINEGAR**

1 clove **GARLIC**

1 teaspoon minced **FRESH GINGER**

½ teaspoon crushed **RED CHILE FLAKES**

Preheat the oven to 400 degrees F.

Place the garbanzo beans on a Silpat mat or a baking sheet lined with parchment paper, and bake until golden brown, 30 to 35 minutes. (Alternatively, you can air fry them at 400 degrees F for 20 minutes.)

Place the cooked beans in a high-powered blender with the remaining ingredients and process, using the blender tamper to combine the ingredients evenly. The mixture will emulsify quickly and thicken. Add more water if the mixture becomes too thick to move, blending well after each addition.

> **CHEF'S NOTES:** It is very important that you always roast the beans first. It is the roasting that makes this delicious sauce taste like a Thai peanut sauce.
>
> A high-power blender will warm the sauce for serving over veggies or over grain and veggie bowls.
>
> When you refrigerate the sauce, it will become even thicker and be a great dipping sauce for oven roasted French fries or sweet potato fries.

savory soups

10

Garden Gazpacho

This reminds me of my favorite gazpacho from Café Marmalade.

2 CARROTS

1 YELLOW BELL PEPPER

1 CUCUMBER, peeled and seeded

½ **RED ONION**

8 ROMA TOMATOES

2 cloves **GARLIC**

Juice of 2 **LIMES**

½ cup chopped **CILANTRO**

¼ cup chopped **ITALIAN PARSLEY**

Pinch **CUMIN**

Pinch **CAYENNE PEPPER**

AVOCADO cubes, for garnish

In a food processor fitted with the "S" blade, process each vegetable separately until desired size is reached. I like to vary the texture, so I will chop the carrots very fine and make the other vegetables larger by increments. If you prefer your soup less chunky, you can juice the tomatoes separately through a juicer.

Mix all the ingredients together in a bowl, and chill for at least 4 hours. Season to taste and garnish each serving with cubes of avocado, if desired.

CHEF'S NOTES: I like to add chipotle powder to mine to make it hotter.

Dream of Tomato Soup

A much healthier version of a childhood favorite with a twist. Reminiscent of Campbell's Cream of Tomato Soup

1 pound **ROMA TOMATOES**, chopped

2 **RED BELL PEPPERS**, seeded

1 clove **GARLIC**

6 to 8 large **BASIL** leaves

Juice of 1 **LEMON**

¾ cup oil-free, salt-free **SUN-DRIED TOMATOES** (about 3 ounces)

¼ teaspoon **CHIPOTLE POWDER**, or more, to taste

1 cup shelled **HEMP SEEDS**

Place all the ingredients except the hemp seeds in a high-powered blender and process until smooth. (Using a high-powered blender will warm the soup.) Add the hemp seeds and blend again until creamy.

> **CHEF'S NOTES:** This is also delicious over pasta or steamed veggies.
>
> For a reduced-fat version, substitute one (15-ounce) can cannellini beans or 1½ cups cooked beans for the hemp seeds.

Popeye's Perfection

1 cup water or unsweetened **NONDAIRY MILK**

12 ounces **BABY ORGANIC SPINACH**

1 small **SHALLOT**

1 large **DATE**, soaked, or more, to taste

1 cup ripe **AVOCADO**

2 tablespoons fresh **LEMON JUICE**

3 ounces oil-free, salt-free **SUN-DRIED TOMATOES**

HEMP SEEDS for garnish

Place the water or nondairy milk and the sun-dried tomatoes in a high-powered blender and process until dissolved. Add the spinach, shallot, and date and process again until smooth. Add the avocado and lemon juice and blend briefly until smooth. Sprinkle with hemp seeds, if desired. Enjoy immediately.

Easy Edamame Soup

With tofu, miso and edamame, this soup has triple the soy power!

12 cups **WATER** or sodium-free **VEGETABLE STOCK**

4 cups **BROCCOLI** florets

4 cups shelled **EDAMAME**

1 pound **TOFU**, cubed

2 bunches **SCALLIONS**

6 tablespoons low-sodium **MISO**

2 cloves **GARLIC**, or more, to taste

1 (2-inch) piece **GINGER**

Bring the water or stock to a boil in a large soup, pot. Add the tofu, broccoli, and edamame, and return to a boil. Simmer for 4 to 5 minutes, until the vegetables are bright green and crisp. Squeeze the garlic and ginger through a garlic press and add to the soup. Dissolve the miso separately in 1 cup liquid from the soup, then blend into soup.

Creamy Corn Chowder

I prefer this soup served cold like a gazpacho.

2½ cups unsweetened **NONDAIRY MILK**

2½ cups **CORN KERNELS**

1 small **SHALLOT**

1 **AVOCADO**

CILANTRO, diced **AVOCADO**, **CORN KERNELS**, for garnish

Puree all ingredients in a high-powered blender until smooth. Ladle into bowls and sprinkle with cilantro, diced avocado, and corn kernels.

> **CHEF'S NOTES:** You can defrost frozen corn or use fresh corn for this super easy soup.
>
> It's also great with a little chipotle powder.

Nutrient-Rich Black Bean Soup

No one will guess that there are two pounds of greens hidden in this delicious and easy-to-make soup. There is no need to cut anything up as the soup will be blended. If you are using salt-free beans, it is not even necessary to rinse or drain them.

12 cups water or salt-free **VEGETABLE BROTH**

6 (15-ounce) cans salt-free **BLACK BEANS**

2 (16-ounce) bags frozen **CORN**

8 cloves **GARLIC**

2 **RED ONIONS**

2 large **SWEET POTATOES**, peeled if not organic

1 pound **BABY BOK CHOY** (approximately 3 heads)

1 pound **MUSHROOMS**

¾ cup oil-free, salt-free **SUN-DRIED TOMATOES** (about 3 ounces)

1 pound **GREENS** (kale, collard, mustard, chard, or a combination)

2 tablespoons **CUMIN**

2 tablespoons **OREGANO**

1 tablespoon **SMOKED PAPRIKA**

1 teaspoon **CHIPOTLE POWDER**

Zest of 1 **LIME** (optional)

½ cup **LIME JUICE**

Place the water or broth in a large soup pot and bring to a boil. Reduce the heat and add the beans, one pound of the corn, the garlic, onions, sweet potatoes, bok choy, mushrooms, sun-dried tomatoes, and greens. Simmer uncovered for 30 minutes.

Remove from the heat and blend the soup with an immersion blender, or carefully process in a blender, one to two cups at a time, until pureed. Stir in the cumin, oregano, chipotle powder, lime zest (if using), lime juice, and remaining pound of corn.

CHEF'S NOTES: For more texture, you can also set aside half the beans (3 cans) and stir them in whole after the soup is blended.

Garnish with pepitas and cilantro, if desired.

This makes a lot of soup. The recipe can be cut in half and made in an Instant Pot. It also freezes well.

Cream of Zucchini Soup

Start eating this soup made from zucchini and soon you'll fit into your bikini!

1½ pounds **ZUCCHINI, cut up** (about 3)

12 ounces unsweetened **HEMP MILK**

1 clove **GARLIC** (or more, to taste)

3 tablespoons fresh **LEMON JUICE**

4 large **BASIL** leaves

4 pitted **DATES**

½ cup **HEMP SEEDS**

SPROUTS or **ZUCCHINI CUBES**, for garnish

Place all the ingredients in a high-powered blender and process until smooth. Garnish with small cubes of zucchini or sprouts, if desired. Enjoy immediately. Delicious served warm or cold.

CHEF'S NOTES: If you can't find hemp milk, unsweetened almond milk works very well.

For a reduced-fat version, omit the hemp seeds and add one (15-ounce) can cannellini beans.

Tomato and Tortilla Soup

4 cups **RED ONION**, finely diced

6 cloves **GARLIC**, minced or put through a garlic press

4 (14.5-ounce) cans salt-free diced **TOMATOES**

4 cups **WATER**

1 tablespoon **CHILI POWDER**

12 small oil-free, salt-free corn **TORTILLAS**, cut into sixths

¼ cup fresh **LIME JUICE**

AVOCADO and **CILANTRO**, for garnish

Sauté the onions in a little water in a soup pot for 8 to 10 minutes, until soft and translucent. Add the garlic and cook for another 2 to 3 minutes.

Add the tomatoes and water and bring to a boil. Add the chili powder. Reduce the heat and add the tortilla pieces. Cover and simmer for 12 to 15 minutes, until the tortillas are soft and broken down.

Remove from the heat and stir in lime juice. Garnish with sliced avocado and cilantro, if desired.

CHEF'S NOTES: Normally, you would use a roux made from butter, flour, and cream to thicken a soup. The corn tortillas do the same thing as they break down, giving the soup a creamy texture and mouth feel but in a more healthful way.

Stompin' at the Savoy Cabbage Soup

This delicious soup is a healthier version of the sweet and sour cabbage soup my Russian grandmother would make on Friday nights. It's so good that it would even make Louis Armstrong stomp!

2 large **YELLOW ONIONS**, diced (about 4 cups)

1 cup **CARROTS**, sliced

1 cup **CELERY**, diced

6 cloves **GARLIC**, pressed

1 pound **CREMINI MUSHROOMS**, sliced

8 cups **WATER**

2 (14.5 ounce) **cans salt-free DICED TOMATOES**

1 (6 ounce) **can salt-free TOMATO PASTE**

1 head **SAVOY CABBAGE**, shredded (about 10 cups)

1 cup **FRESH BASIL**, cut into ribbons

4 tablespoons **APPLE CIDER VINEGAR**

Sauté the onions in a little water until translucent and soft, about 8 to 10 minutes. Add the carrots, celery, garlic, and mushrooms, and sauté another 8 to 10 minutes, until the carrots are soft.

Add the water, diced tomatoes, and tomato paste, and bring to a boil. Add the shredded cabbage, reduce the heat, and cook for a few more minutes, until the cabbage becomes slightly softened. I only cook it 2 to 3 more minutes because I like my cabbage to have a slight crunch, but you can cook it longer if you prefer. Remove from the heat and stir in the basil and vinegar.

> **CHEF'S NOTES:** Savoy cabbage is a very pretty cabbage available at most supermarkets. If you can't find it, feel free to substitute Napa cabbage, regular cabbage, or even kale.

Sweet Potato Soup with Cannellini Beans and Rainbow Chard

The preparation for this soup can be done in advance. You can have the leeks sliced, the sweet potatoes diced, the beans rinsed, the chard chopped, the juice squeezed, and the water measured out. Then it takes only 20 minutes to cook. This recipe can easily be doubled.

8 cups water or low-sodium **VEGETABLE BROTH**

2 **LEEKS** (approximately 6 ounces), **thinly sliced**

2 or 3 large **SWEET POTATOES** (2 pounds), **peeled and cut into uniform cubes**

2 (15-ounce) cans **CANNELLINI BEANS** (or 3 cups cooked beans), **rinsed and drained**

¾ cup oil-free, salt-free **SUNDRIED TOMATOES** (about 3 ounces)

1 pound **RAINBOW CHARD**, chopped

¼ cup fresh squeezed **LEMON JUICE**, plus zest

Chopped **ITALIAN PARSLEY** and fresh **LEMON TWIST**, for garnish

In a large soup pot, bring the water or vegetable broth to a boil. Reduce the heat to medium and add the leeks. Cook for about 8 minutes, until soft.

Add the cubed sweet potatoes and cook for another 8 to 10 minutes, until tender. Add the beans and sun-dried tomatoes and cook for an additional 2 minutes.

Remove the soup pot from the heat and stir in the chard so that it wilts. Stir in the lemon juice and zest. Top with chopped Italian parsley, if desired, and garnish with a fresh lemon twist.

> **CHEF'S NOTES:** With the bright orange sweet potatoes, white beans, and rainbow-colored chard, this is a very pretty soup. If you can't find rainbow chard, feel free to substitute Swiss chard or any greens such as collards, spinach, or kale.
>
> You can also make this soup with butternut squash or white potatoes in place of the sweet potatoes.

sensational sides & zesty sidekicks

11

Garlic Hasselback Potatoes

Named for the Swedish restaurant Hasselbacken, where they were created in 1953, these potatoes quickly gained in popularity throughout Sweden. Acclaimed for their tender interior and crispy, crunchy exterior, their renown soon spread worldwide. Greasy, salt-laden potato chips ain't got nothin' on these!

Large russet POTATOES

Peeled GARLIC cloves, very thinly sliced

Preheat the oven to 425 degrees F.

Cut each potato about halfway through into thin, fan-like slices. Take care not to cut all the way through the bottom of the potatoes. Insert one garlic slice in between each potato slice.

Place the potatoes on a baking sheet and bake for 1 hour, or until crisp on the outside and tender on the inside. Peel, eat, and repeat.

> **CHEF'S NOTES:** You can thinly slice the garlic most easily using a mandolin. (For safety, always wear a glove when using a mandolin.)
>
> For extra crispiness, put the cooked potatoes in an air fryer at 400 degrees F for a few minutes.

Turnip or Rutabaga Fries   *NEW!*

Even though I recommend a starch-based diet, it's nice to also be able to make fries from non-starchy vegetables. Because of the color of the rutabagas, people actually think they are eating fries made from Yukon gold potatoes, so this could be a great way to get your kids to eat more non-starchy veggies.

TURNIPS or RUTABAGAS (or both)

Preheat the oven to 400 degrees F.

Cut the turnips and rutabagas into French fries. Place them on a baking sheet covered with a Silpat mat, nonstick silicone baking mat, or piece of parchment paper, and bake for 30 minutes, until crisp. You can also air fry them at 400 degrees F for 20 minutes. Serve with your favorite condiment.

Waffle Hash Browns

1 pound frozen, shredded **HASH BROWNS**, defrosted

Preheat a nonstick waffle iron.

Squeeze out the excess liquid from the defrosted hash browns. (You can use a nut milk or paint straining bag to help.) Carefully and evenly place the shredded potatoes on the waffle iron. Close and cook for 15 minutes or more, until the desired level of crispness is reached. Enjoy immediately.

Miso Collards with a Kick

Thank you, Jetta Mason, for sharing this recipe.

2 bunches **COLLARD GREENS**

3 cloves **FRESH GARLIC**, diced fine or pressed

½ large **BROWN** or **YELLOW ONION**, sliced thin

1 to 2 tablespoons diced **JALAPEÑO CHILES**

1 cup thinly sliced **CARROTS**

2 tablespoons low-sodium **MISO**, dissolved in ¾ cup water

Reduced **BALSAMIC VINEGAR** (optional)

Cut the stem from each collard leaf like a V and chop the leaves into medium pieces.

Over medium heat, sauté the garlic, onions, and chiles in a little water in a heavy nonstick saucepan until the onions are translucent. Add the carrots and sauté for a few minutes. Add the miso and water mixture and allow to thicken slightly, stirring frequently.

Place the collards on top, cover, and turn down the heat. You can drizzle a little balsamic vinegar on top of collards before covering. When the collards start to wilt, stir everything together, and cook for another 5 to 10 minutes.

CHEF'S NOTES: If you are avoiding all sodium, omit the miso.

Date-Glazed Brussels Sprouts

Even people who say they don't normally like Brussels sprouts will enjoy this dish.

1½ pounds **BRUSSELS SPROUTS**

¼ cup finely minced **SHALLOTS**

¼ cup **DATE SYRUP**

1 tablespoon low-sodium **TAMARI**

1 tablespoon Westbrae salt-free **DIJON MUSTARD**

1 tablespoon **ARROWROOT POWDER**

Finely diced **RED BELL PEPPER** and **NUTS** (optional)

Cut off the stems from the Brussels sprouts and slice the sprouts in half. Cook in boiling water for 2 minutes, drain, and rinse in cold water. (This step can be done in advance.)

In a heavy nonstick saucepan, sauté the shallots in a few tablespoons of broth or water for 2 to 3 minutes, adding more liquid as needed. Add the Brussels sprouts and sauté for 4 minutes.

Whisk together the date syrup, tamari, Dijon mustard, and arrowroot. Pour over the vegetables and cook for 2 minutes, until the sauce has thickened. Garnish with red bell pepper or nuts, if desired.

CHEF'S NOTES: If you are avoiding all sodium, substitute any reduced balsamic vinegar for the tamari.

Quick Dijon Balsamic-Glazed Brussels Sprouts

NEW!

This is a quicker and easier version of the recipe that was created by my friend Zena and first appeared in my book _The Secrets to Ultimate Weight Loss._ By using frozen veggies and an air fryer, the prep time has been cut in half.

  1 tablespoon stone-ground **MUSTARD**, plus more to taste

  1 tablespoon California Balsamic Smoked **HICKORY VINEGAR** or flavor of your choice, plus more to taste

  1 (16-ounce) bag frozen **BRUSSELS SPROUTS**

Combine the mustard and vinegar in a very small bowl.

  Cook the Brussels sprouts using your preferred method (steam, boil, or microwave). Drain well and air fry at 400 degrees F until crispy, about 15 to 20 minutes.

  Transfer to a bowl, add the mustard mixture, and toss until evenly distributed. Add more mustard or vinegar as desired.

CHEF'S NOTES: If you have a Trader Joe's near you, try their frozen baby Brussels sprouts, as they are very tender and aren't bitter.

If you don't like mustard, replace it with 2 tablespoons reduced balsamic vinegar in the flavor of your choice.

Pineapple Unfried Rice

A great way to use leftover brown rice

1 (20-ounce) can crushed unsweetened **PINEAPPLE**

1 **RED BELL PEPPER**, finely diced

1 bunch **SCALLIONS**

1 cup **GREEN PEAS**

4 ounces **PEA PODS**, sliced

4 cups chilled cooked **BROWN RICE**

½ cup low-sodium **TAMARI**

1 bunch **CILANTRO LEAVES**, chopped

Drain the can of pineapple, reserving the juice to use to sauté the veggies.

Heat ½ cup of the juice in a wok or nonstick skillet over medium-high heat. Add the pepper and scallions and sauté 2 to 3 minutes. Add the peas, pea pods and rice and cook for another 2 to 3 minutes. Add the pineapple and tamari and cook for another minute or so. If the mixture becomes too dry, add more pineapple juice as you are sautéing. Remove from the heat, stir in the cilantro, and serve.

> **CHEF'S NOTES:** For a spectacular presentation, serve in a hollowed-out fresh pineapple half.
>
> If you are avoiding all sodium, substitute ½ cup California Balsamic Teriyaki vinegar for the tamari.

Spanish "Rice"

Grated cauliflower resembles rice. You can now buy riced cauliflower in the freezer section of many supermarkets. Try using an orange cauliflower if they're available in your area.

1 head **CAULIFLOWER**	½ cup chopped **CILANTRO**
4 **SCALLIONS**, sliced	2 **AVOCADOS**, mashed
2 **TOMATOES**, diced	1 tablespoon **PAPRIKA**
1 **ORANGE BELL PEPPER**, diced	1 teaspoon **CHILI POWDER**
2 tablespoons fresh **LEMON JUICE**	1 **JALAPEÑO CHILE**, diced (optional)

In a food processor fitted with the grating blade, grate the cauliflower. Place in a bowl and mix in the remaining ingredients by hand.

CHEF'S NOTES: If you want your dish less spicy, omit the seeds from the chile.

Make sure you wear gloves when cutting hot chiles and never touch your eyes!

Mashed Notatoes

If you serve this with gravy, no one will know it isn't potatoes.

1 head **CAULIFLOWER**

NUTRITIONAL YEAST or **FAUX PARMESAN** (page 127)

Steam or blanch the cauliflower until soft. Place in a food processor fitted with the "S" blade and process until smooth and creamy. Add the nutritional yeast or Faux Parmesan to taste and process again.

CHEF'S NOTES: Don't be surprised if you end up eating the whole head all by yourself!

You can also make this with parsnips.

Oven-Roasted Caramelized Onions

Thank you, Zel Allen, author of *The Nut Gourmet,* for allowing me to share this ingenious recipe. Zel's website is vegparadise.com and her blog is nutgourmet.wordpress.com.

3 medium **ONIONS**, sliced about ⅜ inch thick

1 teaspoon **BALSAMIC VINEGAR**

1 teaspoon low-sodium **TAMARI**

Preheat the oven to 375 degrees F.

Double stack the onions onto the center of a jellyroll pan and roast them for 15 minutes. Using a spatula, turn the onions over, piling them into the center of the pan, and roast for another 15 minutes. Turn the onions again and separate them into a single layer. Roast for 10 minutes longer.

Add the balsamic vinegar and tamari and mix well with the spatula. Spread the onions into a single layer and roast for another 10 minutes.

CHEF'S NOTES: If you are avoiding all sodium, replace the tamari with 2 teaspoons balsamic vinegar.

Quinoa Salad with Currants, Pistachios, and Pomegranate

Try red quinoa for a colorful change of pace.

1 (16-ounce) box **QUINOA**, cooked and cooled

1 cup **LIME JUICE**, plus zest if using fresh limes

2 ounces finely chopped **SCALLIONS**

2 ounces finely chopped **ITALIAN PARSLEY**

2 ounces finely chopped **MINT**

2 cups **DRIED CURRANTS**

8 ounces raw **PISTACHIOS**

1 cup **POMEGRANATE SEEDS**

Prepare the quinoa according to the package directions. Place in a large bowl and allow to cool.

Juice and zest the limes if using fresh limes. Pour over the quinoa. Add the remaining ingredients and mix well. Chill.

CHEF'S NOTES: Try substituting orange juice and orange zest for the lime or unsweetened cherries for the currants.

For a reduced-fat version, omit the nuts.

For a lower-calorie option, substitute 2 cups fresh blueberries for the dried currants.

Spicy Peanut Noodles with Broccoli

This reminds me of the peanut noodles from Chin Chin, a group of West Coast restaurants. If you don't want to use traditional noodles, you try vegetable "noodles" made from spiralized zucchini, sweet potato, or butternut squash. You can also buy pasta in a variety of shapes and sizes made from hearts of palm, legumes, sweet potatoes, or zucchini.

1 pound your favorite **NOODLES**

1 pound **BROCCOLI** florets

¾ cup unsweetened, unsalted **PEANUT BUTTER**

¾ cup **WATER**

¼ cup **RICE VINEGAR**

2 tablespoons low-sodium **TAMARI**

2 tablespoons **DATE SYRUP**

2 cloves **GARLIC**, pressed

¼ to ½ ounce piece **FRESH GINGER**, pressed

½ teaspoon **RED PEPPER FLAKES**

8 **SCALLIONS**, thinly sliced on the diagonal

SESAME SEEDS or chopped unsalted **PEANUTS** for garnish

Cook the pasta according to the package directions. Run under cold water when done. Drain and place in a large bowl.

Blanch the broccoli and run under cold water when done. Drain and add to the pasta along with the scallions.

To make the sauce, combine the peanut butter, water, rice vinegar, tamari, date syrup, garlic, ginger, and red pepper in a saucepan over medium-high heat. Whisk until smooth and cook for about 10 minutes, until thickened.

Pour the sauce over the noodles and broccoli and thoroughly combine. Chill before serving and top with sesame seeds or unsalted peanuts, if desired.

CHEF'S NOTES: If you are avoiding all sodium, substitute 2 tablespoons California Balsamic Teriyaki vinegar for the tamari.

For a reduced-fat version, substitute salt- and sugar-free powdered almond butter or powdered peanut butter for the fresh peanut butter.

Saucy Glazed Mushrooms

4 cloves **GARLIC**, pressed, or more to taste

2 pounds **MUSHROOMS**, sliced

Low-sodium **TAMARI** or coconut aminos

1 **RED ONION**, finely diced

Place the garlic and mushrooms in a bowl, pour over just enough tamari or coconut aminos to cover, and marinate several hours or overnight. Drain mushrooms, reserving liquid.

Sauté the onion in the leftover tamari or coconut aminos in a nonstick pan until nicely browned, approximately 10 minutes, adding a tablespoon tamari at a time if onion becomes dry. Add the drained mushrooms and sauté until all the liquid has been absorbed and the mushrooms are glazed.

CHEF'S NOTES: This is also delicious over pasta.

If you are avoiding all sodium, replace the tamari with either California Balsamic Gilroy Garlic or Teriyaki vinegar.

Holiday Baked Yams

If I had a nickel for every time someone asked me the difference between a yam and a sweet potato, I could retire. They're both delicious (and I still don't know)!

4 large **YAMS**, peeled and diced

2 ripe **PEARS**, peeled and diced

1 cup unsweetened **DRIED CRANBERRIES**

½ cup fresh **ORANGE JUICE**

1 tablespoon alcohol-free **VANILLA**, or 1 teaspoon **VANILLA POWDER**

Preheat the oven to 350 degrees F.

Mix all the ingredients together and place in a baking dish that has a lid. Cover and bake for one hour or until soft. You should easily be able to pierce the yams with a fork.

Twice-Baked Stuffed Sweet Potatoes

This is so pretty, and it tastes as good as it looks. This recipe is a great way to use leftover cranberry relish.

4 or 5 medium **SWEET POTATOES**

½ cup **5-MINUTE CRANBERRY RELISH** (page 122)

½ cup dried unsweetened **CRANBERRIES**

½ cup chopped **PECANS** (optional)

Bake the sweet potatoes until tender. Cool slightly and cut in half. Scoop the pulp from each potato half, leaving a wall about a ¼-inch thick so the shell can be filled.

Preheat the oven to 350 degrees F. Mash the sweet potatoes with a potato masher and add the cranberry relish and dried cranberries. Mix well to combine. Scoop the sweet potato mixture evenly into the shells. Sprinkle with pecans, if desired. Bake for 30 minutes, or until heated through.

5-Minute Cranberry Relish

Why cook your relish or use sugar when you can make this instead?

2 large ORANGES

1 (12-ounce) **bag fresh CRANBERRIES**

½ **cup pitted DATES, or more to taste**

4 tablespoons CHIA SEEDS

Grate the zest from the oranges, then peel the oranges and discard the peels. In a food processor fitted with the "S" blade, process all the ingredients until the desired chunky texture is reached.

> **CHEF'S NOTES:** This is also delicious on your morning oatmeal.
>
> Add fresh ginger and lime juice for a delicious variation.

Fresh Herb Chutney   *NEW!*

This is delicious over veggies and rice dishes or even just over plain rice.

2 tablespoons WATER

¼ **cup LIME JUICE**

1 (6-ounce) **bag SPINACH** (approximately 6 cups)

1 bunch CILANTRO (about 1 cup, packed)

1 cup FRESH MINT

4 deglet noor DATES (about 1 ounce)

1 SERRANO CHILE (2 if you prefer it hotter)

4 cloves GARLIC

½ **ounce FRESH GINGER** (about a ½-inch piece)

Place the water and lime juice in a high-powered blender. Add the spinach and blend until smooth. Add the remaining ingredients and blend again until smooth.

Zesty Mango Salsa **_NEW!_**

This is similar to traditional Pico de Gallo (page 124) made from tomatoes, but the mango gives it a burst of sweetness and flavor.

  3 cups chopped **MANGO**

  2 cups chopped **RED BELL PEPPER**

  ½ cup chopped **RED ONION**

  1 cup chopped **CILANTRO** leaves

  ¼ to ½ cup **LIME JUICE**

  ½ to 1 **JALAPEÑO CHILE** (optional)

Place the mango, bell pepper, and red onion into a bowl. Add the cilantro leaves and ¼ cup of the lime juice. Taste and add more lime juice to taste. (Frozen, defrosted mango may be sweeter and more watery than fresh mango, and some fresh mangoes will be sweeter than others.) Add the chile if desired.

CHEF'S NOTES: You can use fresh mango, pre-cut packaged mango, or frozen defrosted mango. The consistency will be different depending on which you use.

If you cannot find mango, you can substitute unsweetened canned or fresh pineapple.

The intensity of jalapeño chiles will vary but removing the seeds will lower the heat.

Please use food service gloves when working with hot peppers, as their volatile oils will remain on your fingers for some time. Remove gloves first before you touch your face and eyes.

Pico de Gallo

3 firm **ROMA TOMATOES**

Juice from 1 **LIME**

1 **SHALLOT**

2 cloves **GARLIC**

1 **JALAPEÑO CHILE**

Chopped **CILANTRO**

Cut the tomatoes in half, squeeze out the seeds and any extra juice, and dice. Place in a bowl and add the lime juice.

Dice the shallot and garlic and add to the tomatoes. Finely dice the chile, removing the seeds if you like it less hot. Add to the tomatoes. Season with chopped cilantro, to taste, and stir.

> **CHEF'S NOTES:** Sometimes, I will add a finely diced red bell pepper.

Quickles

These are just like homemade pickles, but quicker to make!

CUCUMBERS

California Balsamic Garden Dill **MUSTARD**
SEED VINEGAR or flavor of your choice

Thinly slice the cucumbers using a knife or mandolin. Add the vinegar to cover and toss until evenly distributed. Cover the bowl and let marinate in the refrigerator for at least 15 minutes before serving.

> **CHEF'S NOTES:** Once you start using the cucumbers, you can keep adding more slices to the marinade in the bowl as often as you like.
>
> For safety, always wear a glove when using a mandolin.

Pickled Onions

Put a few of these on top of any salad to take it from bland to grand!

ONIONS

California Balsamic Ruby **RED ONION**
VINEGAR or other flavor of your choice

Thinly slice the onions with a knife or mandolin and transfer to a bowl. Add enough vinegar to cover and toss until evenly distributed. Cover the bowl and marinate in the refrigerator for 8 to 12 hours.

> **CHEF'S NOTES:** Once you start using the onions, you can add more to the bowl as often as you like. You also can add other veggies and let them marinate along with the onions.
>
> For safety, always wear a glove when using a mandolin.

Easy Cheesy Peasies

1 pound frozen **PEAS**, defrosted

1 cup raw **CASHEWS**, soaked

¼ cup **NUTRITIONAL YEAST FLAKES**

¼ cup low-sodium **MISO**

¼ cup fresh **LEMON JUICE**

¼ cup **WATER**

4 cloves **GARLIC**, or to taste

¼ teaspoon **RED CHILE FLAKES**

½ teaspoon **TURMERIC**

Place the defrosted peas in a serving bowl. Drain and rinse the cashews.

Place all the ingredients, except for the peas, in a food processor fitted with the "S" blade and combine until smooth. Pour over the peas and mix well. Chill well before serving.

If you are avoiding all sodium, omit the miso.

CHEF'S NOTES: For a reduced-fat version, substitute one (15-ounce) can cannellini beans or 1½ cups cooked beans for the cashews.

Roasted Garbanzos Italiano *NEW!*

A yummy unprocessed alternative to croutons.

- 1 (15-ounce can) **GARBANZO BEANS** or 1½ cups of cooked garbanzo beans
- ¼ cup California Balsamic 7-Herb **ITALIAN VINEGAR**

Rinse and drain garbanzo beans. Add the vinegar and mix well. Let marinate for a few hours, until most of the vinegar is absorbed.

Air fry at 400 degrees F for 20 minutes (or until desired level of crunchiness is reached), or roast in an oven at 400 degrees F for 30 minutes.

> **CHEF'S NOTES:** If you don't have the California Balsamic brand vinegar, use another brand of white balsamic vinegar and add 1 tablespoon Italian seasoning.

Faux Parmesan

This is much more economical than the store-bought version. We use this as a topping on chili and soup and on everything from air-popped popcorn and potatoes to steamed veggies.

- 1 cup raw **ALMONDS** or **CASHEWS**
- ½ cup **NUTRITIONAL YEAST FLAKES**
- 1 tablespoon salt-free **SEASONING** (I prefer Benson's Table Tasty)

In a food processor fitted with the "S" blade or in a blender, combine all the ingredients until a powdery texture is achieved. If you like it chunkier, process it less.

> **CHEF'S NOTES:** You can also use store-bought almond flour in place of the almonds.
>
> For a reduced-fat version, substitute ½ cup rolled oats for the nuts.

decadent desserts

12

Berried Treasures

My friend Tim Ray loves these even more than chocolate!

CRUST

2 cups raw **WALNUTS**

2 cups pitted **DATES**

FILLING

2 pounds frozen **BLUEBERRIES**, defrosted

1 pound **DATES**, soaked in 16 ounces orange juice

Zest and juice of one **LEMON** (about ¼ cup juice)

4 tablespoons **CHIA SEEDS**

1 recipe **STREUSEL TOPPING** (page 145)

To make the crust, process the walnuts into a powder in a food processor fitted with the "S" blade, being careful not to overprocess and turn them into nut butter. Add the dates a few at a time until the mixture sticks together, and you can easily roll it into a ball.

To make the filling, puree the blueberries and dates in a food processor fitted with the "S" blade until smooth. Add the lemon juice and zest and chia seeds and process again briefly.

Press the crust into the bottom of an 8-inch square springform pan. Pour the filling over crust and sprinkle the streusel topping over the filling. (Reserve any extra topping to sprinkle on fresh fruit.) Chill until firm and cut into squares before serving.

CHEF'S NOTES: Substitute blackberries or raspberries for all or some of the blueberries.

These freeze well and are also delicious warmed.

For an extra-decadent treat, serve with Macadamia Nut Crème (page 147) or Pear Crème Anglais (page 147).

Cherried Treasures

Frozen cherries aren't always available, so when you see them, be sure to stock up.

CRUST

2 cups raw **WALNUTS**

1 cup pitted **DATES**

1 cup dried unsweetened **CHERRIES**

FILLING

2 pounds frozen **CHERRIES**, defrosted

1 pound **DATES**, soaked in 16 ounces orange juice

Zest and juice from two **LIMES** (approximately ¼ cup juice.)

4 tablespoons **CHIA SEEDS**

1 recipe **STREUSEL TOPPING** (page 145)

To make the crust, process the walnuts into a powder in a food processor fitted with the "S" blade, being careful not to overprocess and turn them into nut butter. Add the 1 cup dates and dried cherries a few at a time and process until the mixture sticks together and you can easily roll it into a ball.

To make the filling, puree the cherries and 1 pound dates in a food processor fitted with the "S" blade until smooth. Add the lime juice and zest and chia seeds, and process again briefly.

Press the crust into the bottom of an 8-inch square springform pan. Pour the cherry filling over the crust and sprinkle the streusel topping over the filling. (Reserve any extra topping to sprinkle on fresh fruit.) Chill until firm and cut into squares before serving.

CHEF'S NOTES: When you buy dried fruit, always look for a brand that's not only free of added sugar and oil, but also sulfites, which are often used as preservatives. Sulfites can trigger asthma or migraines in people who are sensitive to those substances.

It's also fun to make this a layered dessert by making half the filling with blueberries and the other half with cherries. Start with the blueberry layer and top with the with cherry layer!

You can also soak the dates in pomegranate juice instead of orange juice.

Cherry Cobbler

This tastes as good as it looks and is also delicious warmed in the dehydrator.

FILLING

3 (16-ounce bags) frozen **CHERRIES**, defrosted and drained (juice reserved)

1 cup pitted **DATES**, soaked in the cherry juice

Juice and rind of 1 **LEMON**

1 tablespoon alcohol-free **VANILLA EXTRACT**, or 1 teaspoon **VANILLA POWDER**

1 recipe **STREUSEL TOPPING** (page 145)

To make the filling, process about ¼ of the cherries with the rest of the filling ingredients in a food processor fitted with the "S" blade. Stir this mixture into the remaining cherries by hand. Chill 1 hour or until firm.

Assemble in individual glasses, alternately layering the cherry filling with the streusel topping. (Martini glasses make for a beautiful presentation.) Top with Macadamia Nut Crème (page 147).

CHEF'S NOTES: Substitute fresh or frozen peaches for all or some of the cherries.

Mint Chocolate Mousse Torte

A healthier version of the Frango Mint Pie I ate as a child at Marshall Field's in Chicago.

FILLING

16 ounces pitted **DATES**, soaked in 2 cups unsweetened nondairy milk

1 tablespoon alcohol-free **VANILLA EXTRACT**, or 1 teaspoon **VANILLA POWDER**

1 to 2 teaspoons **PEPPERMINT EXTRACT** (depending on how minty you like it)

½ cup **COCOA POWDER** or **CAROB POWDER**

12 ounces **WALNUTS**

½ cup unsweetened **COCONUT**

CRUST

2 cups raw **WALNUTS**

¼ cup **COCOA POWDER** or **CAROB POWDER**

2 cups pitted **DATES**

1 tablespoon alcohol-free **VANILLA**, or 1 teaspoon **VANILLA POWDER**

1 teaspoon **PEPPERMINT EXTRACT**

½ cup **CACAO NIBS**, for garnish

To make the filling, process the soaked dates with the vanilla and peppermint extract in a food processor fitted with the "S" blade until very smooth. Add the cocoa powder and process again until smooth, then place the entire mixture in a bowl.

In the same processor bowl, process the 12 ounces of walnuts until like nut butter. Add the coconut and process again. Add to the date mixture and combine the ingredients by hand until completely incorporated.

To make the crust, process the 2 cups of walnuts with the cocoa or carob powder in a powder in a food processor fitted with the "S" blade. Do not overprocess or you will have nut butter. Add the 2 cups dates, a few at a time, until the mixture holds together and you can easily roll it into a ball. Add the vanilla and peppermint extracts and process again briefly.

Press the crust into an 8- or 9-inch springform pan. Spread the filling over the top, garnish with the cacao nibs, and freeze until solid.

Orange Chocolate Mousse Torte

This is the first recipe I created after culinary school, and it was sold at Santé Restaurant, where I was the executive vegan pastry chef.

HAVE READY:

BASIC HEALTHY PIE CRUST (page 144) made with ¼ cup cocoa powder

FILLING

16 ounces pitted **DATES**, soaked in 2 cups orange juice until soft

12 ounces **WALNUTS**

½ cup **COCOA POWDER** or **CAROB POWDER**

½ cup unsweetened **COCONUT**

1 tablespoon alcohol-free **VANILLA EXTRACT**, or 1 teaspoon **VANILLA POWDER**

½ cup **CACAO NIBS** and **FLAKED COCONUT**, for garnish

To make the filling, drain the dates and process with the vanilla extract or powder in a food processor fitted with the "S" blade until very smooth. Add the cocoa or carob powder and process again until smooth. Place in a bowl.

Using the same processor bowl, process the walnuts into nut butter. Add the coconut and process again. Add this to the date mixture and stir well by hand until the ingredients are completely incorporated.

Press out the crust as desired, pour the filling over the crust, and freeze until firm. Garnish with cacao nibs and flaked coconut.

CHEF'S NOTES: I prefer to make this in a springform pan and serve it with Raspberry Coulis (page 149).

Banana-Strawberry Mousse Tart

This is equally delicious when made with carob powder, and using vanilla powder gives it an extra kick.

CRUST

1 cup raw **CASHEWS** or **MACADAMIA NUTS**

1 cup unsweetened **DRIED COCONUT**

2 cups pitted **DATES**

1 tablespoon alcohol-free **VANILLA**

1 teaspoon **VANILLA POWDER** (optional)

FILLING

2 large ripe **AVOCADOS**

⅓ cup **COCOA POWDER** or **CAROB POWDER**

1 cup **DATE PASTE**, or to taste (page 146)

1 tablespoon alcohol-free **VANILLA**, or 1 teaspoon **VANILLA POWDER**

Sliced ripe **BANANAS** and **STRAWBERRIES**

To make the crust, process the nuts into a powder in a food processor fitted with the "S" blade. Add the coconut and process again. Add enough dates that the mixture will hold together when formed into a ball. Add the vanilla and process again. Press the mixture evenly onto the bottom of a fluted tart pan.

To make the filling, process the avocado, cocoa powder, date paste, and vanilla until smooth in a food processor fitted with the "S" blade. Spread half the filling over the crust and place sliced bananas on top. Layer the other half of the filling over the bananas and place sliced strawberries on top. Chill and serve with Raspberry Coulis (page 149).

> **CHEF'S NOTES:** For a lower-fat crust, substitute 2 cups oats for the coconut and nuts.

Chocolate FUNdue

I created this dip to get my friend's 4-year-old to eat fruit.

1 cup unsweetened, unsalted **PEANUT BUTTER**

1 cup **DATE PASTE** (page 146)

½ cup **COCOA POWDER** or **CAROB POWDER**

1 tablespoon alcohol-free **VANILLA EXTRACT**, or 1 teaspoon **VANILLA POWDER**

¾ to 1 cup unsweetened **NONDAIRY MILK**

Place all the ingredients, except the milk, in a food processor fitted with the "S" blade and process just until they are incorporated, scraping down the sides of the processor bowl if necessary. Slowly add the nondairy milk, a little at a time, until the desired consistency is reached. You can eat this immediately or chill to get a firmer texture.

CHEF'S NOTES: Serve this as a dip with your favorite fruit, such as cut apples or strawberries. Or buy wooden skewers and place several different fruits on them shish-kabob style.

If you have leftover FUNdue, make Nutty Buddies (page 143) or Peanut Butter Fudge Truffles (page 163).

You can make a raw version by using raw almond butter or tahini.

To drastically reduce the fat, my friend Robin replaces half the nut butter with rinsed, drained cannellini beans. You could probably add even more beans and less nut butter, and it would still be delicious.

If you prefer not to use chocolate or carob, omit them, and make a creamy peanut butter dip.

D.B.'s Special

Whoever thought a salad could be a dessert? Well, now it can! This salad was created by "accident" by my friend Michelle Wolf's niece D.B., who put the streusel topping from the Berried Treasures recipe on a salad.

SALAD

FRESH BEETS

CARROTS

APPLES

1 recipe **MANGO-ORANGE SAUCE** (page 149)

STREUSEL TOPPING (page 145)

To make the salad, shred equal amounts of all three ingredients in a food processor fitted with the shredding blade, and place in a large bowl.

Pour the Mango Orange Sauce over the shredded salad and mix well. Top with Streusel Topping.

> **CHEF'S NOTES:** If you don't have a food processor, you could shred all the ingredients by hand. It will just take much longer.

Chocolate-Peanut Butter Nice Cream   *NEW!*

2 tablespoons **PEANUT BUTTER**

2 tablespoons **COCOA POWDER**

2 cups sliced frozen **BANANAS**

½ teaspoon **VANILLA POWDER**, or 1 teaspoon alcohol-free **VANILLA EXTRACT**

Place all the ingredients in a high-powered blender, NutraMilk Nut Processor, or a food processor fitted with the "S" blade, and process until smooth and creamy.

Hockey Pucks

I remember reading in *Prevent and Reverse Heart Disease,* a book by Caldwell B. Esselstyn, Jr., MD, that he eats eight peanut butter cups every New Year's Eve. When I had the honor of having him at my home for dinner, I created this recipe so he could enjoy them more than once a year. I originally called them "Essies" in his honor, but Ann Wheat, co-owner of the amazing Millennium Restaurant in Oakland, renamed them Hockey Pucks because of their shape.

FILLING

1 cup **DATE PASTE** (page 146)

1 cup unsweetened, unsalted **PEANUT BUTTER**

1 tablespoon alcohol-free **VANILLA**, or 1 teaspoon **VANILLA POWDER**

COATING

2 cups unsalted **PEANUTS**

½ cup **COCOA POWDER** or **CAROB POWDER**

2 cups pitted **DATES**

1 tablespoon alcohol-free **VANILLA**, or 1 teaspoon **VANILLA POWDER**

To make the filling, process the date paste, peanut butter, and vanilla in a food processor fitted with the "S" blade until smooth and creamy. Add a little unsweetened almond milk if the mixture does not process easily. Place the filling in a 24-piece silicone brownie pan and freeze until firm.

Prepare the coating by grinding the peanuts into a powder in a food processor fitted with the "S" blade. Add the cocoa or carob powder and process again briefly. Add enough dates until the mixture sticks together and you can form a ball. Add the vanilla and process again.

Place the coating around each frozen peanut butter square and form into a round "hockey puck" with your hands. Store in the freezer.

CHEF'S NOTES: For an all-raw version of these treats, substitute raw almond butter for the peanut butter and raw almonds for the peanuts.

You can find 24-piece silicone brownie pans at wilton.com or on Amazon.

Caramel Blondies

The secret to these healthy but decadent treats are the *white* sweet potatoes. They are very sweet and starchy with a subtle vanilla flavor that makes them taste like cake. Chocolate brownies have nothing on these beauties!

8 ounces pitted **DATES**

8 ounces unsweetened **NONDAIRY MILK**

1 teaspoon **VANILLA POWDER**

2 cups **WHITE SWEET POTATO** flesh (see Chef's Notes below)

1½ cups **ROLLED OATS**

½ cup **MILLET**, ground into flour

2 teaspoons **VANILLA POWDER**

1 teaspoon **CINNAMON**

2 cups mashed **BANANA** (approximately 3)

Reduced-fat **SHREDDED COCONUT**

Create a date paste by soaking the dates in the nondairy milk for several hours or overnight until they are very soft. Place the dates and soaking liquid into a food processor fitted with the "S" blade, add the vanilla powder, and process until smooth. Remove ¾ cup of the date paste and place in the refrigerator to chill while you make the Blondies. This will be your frosting.

Preheated the oven to 350 degrees F. Place the remaining ingredients into the food processor with the remaining date paste, and process until smooth. Pour the batter into a 9-inch square silicone baking pan and bake for 30 to 40 minutes. (The shorter baking time will produce a moister Blondie.) Turn the oven off and allow the pan to cool in the oven.

Once the Blondies are completely cooled, frost with the chilled vanilla date paste. If you like, sprinkle with reduced-fat shredded coconut. Chill and cut into 16 bars.

CHEF'S NOTES: White sweet potatoes are also called Hannah or Jersey yams. They can be found at most natural food stores and ethnic markets. You could also substitute Japanese or Murasaki sweet potatoes which have a purple skin but also have a white flesh. I do not recommend the orange or purple sweet potatoes for this recipe.

Millet helps mitigate the gummy texture of oats. If you don't mind the texture, you can substitute oats for the millet in this recipe.

Snickerdoodles

1 cup ROLLED OATS

½ tablespoon CINNAMON (a really good quality Saigon Cassia preferred)

½ teaspoon VANILLA POWDER

6 ounces pitted DATES (about 1 cup packed)

Preheat the oven to 350 degrees F.

Place the oats, cinnamon, and vanilla in a NutraMilk Nut Processor, and process on "mix" for 1 minute. Add the dates and process on "mix" for 2 minutes, or until a ball forms.

Divide into 6 pieces, roll into balls, and flatten. Bake for 4 minutes on a baking sheet covered with a nonstick silicone baking mat or piece of parchment paper. Flip and bake for 4 minutes more. Remove from the oven and let cool. Store the cookies in a ziplock or other airtight container.

> **CHEF'S NOTES:** You can use another type of food processor, but the processing time will be much longer.
>
> I love the organic, non-irradiated spices from LocalSpicery.com. To get two free small samples, use the code CHEF AJ.

Hot Apple Pie Fries

SLURRY

½ cup **MILLET**, ground into flour

½ cup unsweetened **APPLE JUICE**

½ teaspoon **CINNAMON**

½ teaspoon **VANILLA POWDER**

COATING

1 cup gluten-free **ROLLED OATS**

1 tablespoon **APPLE PIE SPICE**

1 teaspoon **VANILLA POWDER**

1 large **APPLE** cut into "fries" (Use a sweet variety such as Envy or Fuji)

Mix the ingredients for the slurry in a bowl. Combine the ingredients for the coating in a separate bowl.

One at a time, coat each apple "fry" in the slurry and then dredge in the coating. Place on an air fryer tray or basket and air fry at 400 degrees F for about 20 minutes. Serve with Vanilla Caramel Sauce (page 148).

Caramel Apples

When I gave up processed refined sweeteners, I never thought I would be able to enjoy a caramel apple again. Then I created this. Why wait for the fall or Halloween when you can enjoy this healthy treat any time of year? They look just like the real thing and kids of all ages love them!

1 teaspoon **CARAMEL EXTRACT**

DATE PASTE (page 146)

APPLES

CANDY APPLE sticks

Chopped **NUTS, CACAO NIBS,** unsweetened
COCONUT, GOJI BERRIES (optional)

Add 1 teaspoon of caramel extract to the date paste. Place an apple stem side up on a flat surface and push a stick into the core. Roll the apple in the date paste, using your hands to press it if necessary to get the paste to stick. Roll in your favorite topping such as chopped nuts, cacao nibs, unsweetened coconut, goji berries, or a combination. Chill well before serving.

> **CHEF'S NOTES:** Sticks for caramel apples can be found at craft stores or cake decorating stores. If you have trouble finding them, slice the apples into wedges and make individual dipped apple slices.
>
> The streusel topping from Berried Treasures (page 129) also makes a good topping for these.

Nutty Buddies

Tastes just like the frozen bananas from Disneyland, but you won't have to Mickey Mouse around with your health.

  Ripe **BANANAS**, peeled

  CANDY APPLE sticks

  CHOCOLATE FUNDUE (page 136)

  Chopped **NUTS** or unsweetened **COCONUT**

Cut a banana in half and place a stick in the cut end. Coat the banana with the FUNdue, using your hands if necessary to coat evenly. Roll the banana in chopped nuts or unsweetened coconut, place on wax paper, and freeze until hard.

> **CHEF'S NOTES:** If you don't have candy apple sticks, slice the banana and make individual pieces.

Chocolate-Glazed Balsamic Strawberries

A simple, yet elegant, way to prepare dessert.

  2 tablespoons chocolate-infused **BALSAMIC VINEGAR** (such as California Balsamic Chocolate/Orange)

  1 pound **STRAWBERRIES**, stemmed and cut into quarters

  ¼ cup finely chopped **FRESH MINT**

  Sprinkle of **CACAO NIBS**

Pour the vinegar over the sliced strawberries. Add the mint and let marinate for several hours in the refrigerator, stirring occasionally. Distribute among 4 parfait glasses, and sprinkle with cacao nibs before serving.

> **CHEF'S NOTES:** You can also use unflavored balsamic vinegar.

Basic Healthy Pie Crust

Super easy to make and the varieties are endless. It's great just topped with cut-up fresh fruits of any kind. You can even roll the mixture into balls to make healthy cookies. Play around with adding different spices (like cinnamon or nutmeg), different extracts (like vanilla or almond), or the zest and juice of lemons, limes, or oranges.

2 cups raw NUTS

2 cups pitted DATES

In a food processor fitted with the "S" blade, process the nuts until they are a flour-like consistency. Do not overprocess or you will have nut butter.

Add dates, a few at a time, until the mixture clumps together. If you can easily roll a ball from the mixture and it sticks together, you don't need to add any more dates. Press the crust into a pie plate, tarte pan, or springform pan.

> **CHEF'S NOTES:** Substitute raw seeds (such as hemp, sesame, pumpkin, or sunflower) for all or some of the nuts.
>
> Substitute dried fruit (such as apricots, cherries, cranberries, currants, figs, prunes, raisins) for all or some of the dates.
>
> For a lower-fat crust, substitute 2 cups oats for the nuts.

Streusel Topping

I always like to keep some on hand to sprinkle over fresh fruit. This can even turn a sliced banana into a special treat.

1 cup raw **PECANS**

1 cup unsweetened **COCONUT**

2 teaspoons **CINNAMON**

½ teaspoon **NUTMEG**

2 cups pitted **DATES**

In a food processor fitted with the "S" blade, process the nuts into a flour, being careful not to overprocess and turn them into nut butter. Add the coconut, cinnamon, and nutmeg and process again. Add the dates, a few at a time, until a streusel-like texture is achieved. Store in a sealed container in the refrigerator.

CHEF'S NOTES: While the ingredients in the streusel topping are basically the same as those in the Basic Healthy Pie Crust (page 144), we are looking for an entirely different texture. When making a crust, you want everything to stick together and form a ball so that you can press it into a pie pan. When making the streusel topping, you want it more crumbly, so you can sprinkle it over things like a topping.

Some varieties of dates are more moist and sticky than others, so be careful not to add so many that a ball forms (as opposed to when you make a pie crust).

Date Paste

Make sure you always have some of this on hand to create a healthy dessert in no time.

> 1 pound pitted **DATES** (about 2½ cups, pitted)
>
> 1 cup **WATER**, unsweetened **NONDAIRY MILK**, or unsweetened **JUICE**

Soak the dates in the liquid overnight or for several hours, until much of the liquid has been absorbed. In a food processor fitted with the "S" blade, process the dates and liquid until completely smooth. Store Date Paste in the refrigerator.

CHEF'S NOTES: You can add vanilla extract or vanilla powder to your Date Paste if you like.

Date Paste freezes very well.

Date Syrup

Great to use in place of maple syrup.

> Pitted **DATES**
>
> **WATER**

Place the dates in a saucepan and cover with water. Bring the water to a boil and let simmer for 5 minutes. Turn the heat all the way down and continue to simmer for 30 to 60 minutes, until the dates are very soft. Let the mixture cool. Pour into a blender and process until very smooth.

CHEF'S NOTES: You can also purchase date syrup at ilovedatelady.com (use the discount code CHEFAJ).

Macadamia Nut Crème

This is delicious on everything, especially fruit desserts.

> 2 cups **MACADAMIA NUTS**, soaked in enough water
> to cover for at least an hour
>
> **DATE PASTE** (page 146), to taste
>
> 1 tablespoon alcohol-free **VANILLA EXTRACT**,
> or 1 teaspoon **VANILLA POWDER**

In a high-powered blender, process the soaked macadamia nuts, adding as little water as possible and still have the mixture move. Add the Date Paste, the vanilla, and if necessary, add more water to get a thick, but smooth, creamy topping.

> **CHEF'S NOTES:** You can substitute raw cashews for the macadamia nuts.

Pear Crème Anglais

For a delicious variation, you can substitute unsweetened jarred peaches in their own juice for the pears.

> 1 (25-ounce) jar **PEARS**, or 2½ cups pears (if using fresh or canned)
>
> ⅓ cup raw **CASHEWS** or **MACADAMIA NUTS**
>
> 1 tablespoon alcohol-free **VANILLA EXTRACT**, or 1 teaspoon **VANILLA POWDER**

Drain the pears, reserving the juice for another use. In a blender, process the pears until smooth. Add remaining ingredients and blend until incorporated. Chill and serve over any fruit dessert.

> **CHEF'S NOTES:** For a lower-fat option, substitute 1 cup rolled oats for the nuts.

Vanilla Caramel Sauce

Growing up, I so loved the caramel-flavored topping that came in a little jar. Now you can have your Nice Cream and eat it too! This is also great on waffles in place of maple syrup.

8 ounces pitted **DATES**

8 ounces unsweetened **NONDAIRY MILK**

½ teaspoon **VANILLA POWDER**, or more to taste

Soak the dates in the nondairy milk until soft. Process all the ingredients in a high-powered blender until smooth and creamy. Add more nondairy milk if you want it thinner. Pour into a squeeze bottle and refrigerate.

> **CHEF'S NOTES:** If you can find Bahri dates, they naturally taste like caramel. Otherwise, any dates will work.

Wicked Fudge Sauce

This is delicious over fresh banana ice cream made with a juicer or your favorite ice cream machine.

1 cup raw **ALMOND BUTTER**

½ cup **DATE SYRUP**, or more to taste

½ cup **COCOA POWDER** or **CAROB POWDER**

½ cup unsweetened **NONDAIRY MILK**

In a food processor using the "S" blade, process all the ingredients until smooth. If you want a thinner sauce, use more nondairy milk.

> **CHEF'S NOTES:** If you have a dehydrator, try dehydrating the leftover sauce. If you spread it thinly on the Teflex dryer sheets, it will taste like chocolate fruit leather.
>
> If you have a high-powered blender, this will become heated and taste like hot fudge sauce.

Mango-Orange Sauce

A simple dressing for fruit or salad.

8 ounces frozen MANGO, defrosted (or equivalent amount of fresh, ripe mango)

½ cup **ORANGE JUICE**

2 tablespoons fresh LIME JUICE

½ teaspoon **CINNAMON**

Place all dressing ingredients in a high-powered blender and process until smooth.

> **CHEF'S NOTES:** Frozen fruit can be as nutritious as fresh because it is picked at the point of peak ripeness and flash frozen. Keep a variety of frozen fruit on hand in your freezer.

Raspberry Coulis

This sauce is boss!

1 (16-ounce) bag frozen RASPBERRIES, defrosted

DATE PASTE, to taste (page 146)

Alcohol-free **VANILLA EXTRACT** or **ALMOND EXTRACT** (optional)

LEMON JUICE (optional)

Process the raspberries and date paste in a blender until smooth, adding more date paste until the desired sweetness is reached. You can also add a teaspoon of alcohol-free vanilla extract, a dash of alcohol-free almond extract, and a little lemon juice, if desired. Pour into a squeeze bottle and serve over any dessert or use in smoothies.

> **CHEF'S NOTES:** Other frozen fruits, such as cherries or strawberries, are equally delicious. You can also use fresh fruit.

truffles

CHAPTER

Almond Overjoy Balls

Brenda Cohen came in a close second in our truffle-making contest with these.

2 cups raw **ALMONDS**

¼ cup **COCOA POWDER** or **CAROB POWDER**

2 cups pitted deglet noor **DATES**

¼ cup raw **SHREDDED COCONUT** (macaroon cut)

½ cup **GOLDEN RAISINS**

1 tablespoon alcohol-free **VANILLA EXTRACT**, or 1 teaspoon **VANILLA POWDER**

¼ teaspoon alcohol-free **ALMOND EXTRACT** (or to taste)

Equal parts **COCOA** or **CAROB POWDER** and **SHREDDED COCONUT**, for coating

In a food processor fitted with the "S" blade, process the almonds until they are almost the consistency of nut butter. Add the cocoa powder and process again until fully incorporated. Add the dates and process again until the mixture almost holds together. Add the coconut and process again until thoroughly combined. Add raisins and extracts until the mixture will stick together and form a ball if rolled (clumped) in your hand.

Combine the cocoa or carob powder and the shredded coconut into a small bowl. Shape the date and nut mixture into 1-inch balls, using about 1 tablespoon of the mixture per ball. Roll the balls in the cocoa and coconut mixture to coat completely.

Helluva Halvah Bitty Ball

Another delicious recipe from Brenda Cohen (see her Almond Overjoy Balls, page 151), who makes all my recipes better than I do!

½ cup raw **SESAME SEEDS**

2 teaspoons **COCOA POWDER** or **CAROB POWDER**

½ teaspoon **MACA POWDER**

Dash of **CINNAMON**

2 tablespoons **DATE SYRUP**

1 tablespoon raw **TAHINI**

1 teaspoon **VANILLA EXTRACT**, or 1 teaspoon **VANILLA POWDER**

1 tablespoon **CACAO NIBS**

Combine the ingredients one at a time in a food processor fitted with the "S" blade. Process until the mixture holds together. Roll into bitty balls and enjoy!

BRAWnies

2 cups **WALNUTS**

½ cup **COCOA POWDER** or **CAROB POWDER**

2 cups pitted **DATES**

1 tablespoon alcohol-free **VANILLA EXTRACT**, or 1 teaspoon **VANILLA POWDER**

In a food processor fitted with the "S" blade, process the walnuts to the consistency of powder. Do not overprocess into nut butter. Add the cocoa or carob powder and process again. Add the dates, a few at a time, until a ball forms. Add the vanilla and briefly process again. Place into a silicone brownie mold or an 8-inch x 8-inch square pan and freeze until firm.

CHEF'S NOTES: You can use any raw nut or seed (or combination) instead of the walnuts.

For a reduced-fat version, substitute 2 cups rolled oats for the walnuts.

Almond Dream Balls

Nataly Carranza won first place in our truffle-making contest with this recipe.

½ cup raw **ALMONDS**

¼ cup raw **WALNUTS**

½ cup pitted **DATES**

¼ cup raw **ALMOND BUTTER**

½ teaspoon alcohol-free **ALMOND EXTRACT**

SHREDDED COCONUT, for coating

Place the almonds and walnuts into a food processor fitted with the "S" blade and process until coarsely chopped. Add the dates, almond butter, and alcohol-free almond extract, and process until the mixture holds together.

Place the shredded coconut into a small bowl. Shape the date and nut mixture into 1-inch balls, using about 1 tablespoon of the mixture per ball. Roll the balls in the shredded coconut to coat completely.

Apple Pie Hearts

1 cup **ALMONDS**

1 cup **PECANS**

1 cup **WALNUTS**

2 cups sugar-free, sulfite-free **DRIED APPLES**

1 tablespoon **CINNAMON**

¼ to ½ teaspoon **NUTMEG**

2 cups pitted **DATES**

1 tablespoon alcohol-free **VANILLA EXTRACT**,
or 1 teaspoon **VANILLA POWDER**

In a food processor fitted with the "S" blade, grind the nuts to the consistency of flour. Add the dried apples, cinnamon, and nutmeg and process again. Add the dates, a few at a time, until the mixture holds together, then add the vanilla and process briefly. Press into mini heart silicone molds and chill.

CHEF'S NOTES: If you don't have silicone molds, roll the mixture into balls.

For a reduced-fat version, substitute 3 cups rolled oats for the almonds, pecans, and walnuts.

Chocolate Chip Cherry Bites

2 cups raw **PECANS**

½ cup **COCOA POWDER** or **CAROB POWDER**

8 ounces unsweetened, unsulfured **DRIED CHERRIES**

8 ounces pitted **DATES**, plus **DATE SYRUP**, if needed

1 tablespoon alcohol-free **VANILLA EXTRACT**, or 1 teaspoon **VANILLA POWDER**

¼ cup **CACAO NIBS**

In a food processor fitted with the "S" blade, process the nuts to the consistency of flour. Do not overprocess into nut butter. Add the cocoa or carob powder and process again briefly. Add the cherries and process again. Add the dates, a few at a time, until the mixture holds together. Add more dates or a splash of date syrup to get the mixture to this point. Add the vanilla, process briefly, then the cacao nibs and pulse. Press the mixture into a silicone brownie mold or an 8-inch x 8-inch square pan.

CHEF'S NOTES: For a reduced-fat version, substitute 2 cups rolled oats for the pecans.

Figgy Flax

Thank you, Robin Fomalont, for this easy, tasty recipe.

> ½ cup **DATES**
>
> ½ cup **FIGS**
>
> 1 cup raw **CASHEWS**
>
> Toasted **FLAXSEEDS** (for coating)

Combine the dates, figs, and cashews in a food processor fitted with the "S" blade. Form into balls and roll each ball in the toasted flaxseeds.

CHEF'S NOTES: You can use dried figs in place of dates in just about any recipe.

Goji Berry Truffles

These little gems are mostly fruit and contain no nuts.

> ½ cup **HEMP SEEDS**
>
> ½ cup **PUMPKIN SEEDS**
>
> 1 cup **GOJI BERRIES**
>
> ½ cup **DARK RAISINS**
>
> 1½ cups pitted **DATES**
>
> ½ cup **COCOA POWDER** or **CAROB POWDER**
>
> 1 tablespoon alcohol-free **VANILLA EXTRACT**, or 1 teaspoon **VANILLA POWDER**

In a food processor fitted with the "S" blade, grind the hemp and pumpkin seeds into a powder. Add the cocoa/carob powder and combine. Add the goji berries and process again to combine. Add the raisins and dates and process again until the mixture begins to stick together. Add the vanilla and process briefly. Place in a silicone mold or form into balls.

CHEF'S NOTES: For a reduced-fat version, substitute 1½ cups rolled oats for the hemp and pumpkin seeds.

Chocolate Hazelnut Gianduia Truffles

Pronunced "zhahn-DOO-yuh," this recipe is from Michelle Wolf. Her husband, Alan Raz, was the consulting taster!

18 deglet noor pitted **DATES**

Unsweetened **CHOCOLATE ALMOND MILK**

1½ cups raw **HAZELNUTS**

2 tablespoons **COCOA POWDER** or **CAROB POWDER**

½-1 teaspoon alcohol-free **VANILLA EXTRACT**, or 1 teaspoon **VANILLA POWDER**

¼ teaspoon alcohol-free **ALMOND EXTRACT** (optional)

2 dozen whole **HAZELNUTS**

Soften the dates by soaking overnight in some unsweetened chocolate almond milk. Drain. Process ½ cup of the hazelnuts in a food processor fitted with the "S" blade until ground into a coarse powder. Place into a bowl and set aside.

Process the remaining 1 cup hazelnuts in the food processor until ground into a coarse powder. Add the cocoa or carob powder; the soaked, drained dates; and the optional extracts, if using. Process until the mixture becomes a thick paste.

Spoon out the chocolate-nut mixture by rounded teaspoonfuls, one at a time, and place a whole hazelnut into the center of each spoonful. Roll to form small, round balls. Use slightly wet hands to avoid the mixture sticking to your palms.

Roll each ball in the bowl of ground hazelnuts until evenly coated. Store the balls in a tightly covered container in the freezer until ready to serve.

Chocolate-Coated Luscious Lemon Truffle

Kitchen Angel Michelle Wolf brought this over the night the Esselstyns came for dinner. She was quite honored when Ann Esselstyn, a wonderful cook and cookbook author, asked for the recipe.

Note that you'll need to figure in time to soak dates overnight for both the lemon centers and chocolate coating.

LEMON CENTERS

18 deglet noor pitted **DATES**

¼ cup **LEMON JUICE**

2 tablespoons **WATER**

½ cup raw **ALMONDS**

½ cup raw **CASHEWS**

LEMON zest

½ teaspoon **LEMON EXTRACT**

CHOCOLATE COATING

18 deglet noor pitted **DATES**

Unsweetened **CHOCOLATE ALMOND MILK**

1 cup raw **HAZELNUTS** or **PECANS**

¾ cup raw **ALMONDS**

¾ cup **HAZELNUTS**

3 tablespoons **COCOA POWDER** or **CAROB POWDER**

½ to 1 teaspoon alcohol-free **VANILLA EXTRACT**, or 1 teaspoon **VANILLA POWDER**

¼ teaspoon alcohol-free **ALMOND EXTRACT** (optional)

To make the lemon centers, soak the dates overnight in the lemon juice and water. Drain.

Place the almonds and cashews in a food processor fitted with the "S" blade, and grind into a coarse powder. Add the soaked dates, a few at a time, until the mixture holds together. Add the lemon zest and lemon extract and process briefly.

Spoon out the lemon-date mixture by ½ teaspoonfuls, one at a time. Roll to form small, round balls. (Use slightly wet hands to avoid the mixture sticking to your palms.) Place the balls in a container so the balls are not touching. Cover and freeze until the balls are solid.

To make the chocolate coating, soak the dates in unsweetened chocolate almond milk overnight. Drain. Place the 1 cup hazelnuts or pecans in the food processor, and grind into a fine powder. Place into a bowl and set aside.

Place the almonds and ¾ cup hazelnuts into the food processor and grind into coarse powder. Add the cocoa or carob powder, the soaked dates, and extracts, if using. Process until the mixture becomes a thick paste.

To form the truffles, remove the lemon balls from the freezer. Spoon out the chocolate mixture by rounded teaspoonfuls and flatten between your thumbs and first fingers. Place a lemon ball in the center of each piece of chocolate coating and wrap the coating around to enclose. Roll to form round balls. (Use slightly wet hands to avoid the mixture sticking to your palms.)

Roll each ball in the bowl of ground hazelnuts or pecans until evenly coated. Store in a sealed container in the freezer until served.

Tropical Treats

Yi Fan Rao won the very first truffle-making contest with this tasty treat.

1½ cups raw **ALMONDS**

1 cup roughly chopped **MACADAMIA NUTS**

1 cup diced **DRIED PINEAPPLE**

1 cup diced **DRIED APRICOTS**

½ cup roughly chopped raw **ALMONDS**

10 to 12 **DATES**, soaked in water overnight and drained

1 cup golden **FLAX SEEDS**

Grind the raw almonds into a fine meal in a food processor fitted with the "S" blade, and transfer to a large bowl. Add the macadamias, pineapple, apricots, and the ½ cup chopped almonds to the bowl. Chop the dates, add to the bowl, and combine well until the mixture becomes sticky.

Form into 1-inch balls by rolling between the palms of your hands, then roll the balls in the flax seeds to coat them completely. Place the balls in a covered container and freeze. Serve the balls frozen, partly defrosted, or at room temperature.

CHEF'S NOTES: You could also roll them in sesame seeds.

Peanut Bites

2 cups unsalted, roasted **PEANUTS** or **RAW NUTS** of your choice

2 cups pitted **DATES**

1 tablespoon alcohol-free **VANILLA EXTRACT**, or 1 teaspoon **VANILLA POWDER**

In a food processor fitted with the "S" blade, process the nuts until they are the consistency of flour. If using vanilla powder, it can be added with the peanuts. Do not overprocess or you will have nut butter. Add the dates, a few at a time, until the mixture holds together, and you can easily roll a ball that will stick together. If using liquid vanilla extract, add it after the dates, after the mixture has begun to clump together.

> **CHEF'S NOTES:** This is delicious when you mix in some raw cacao nibs.
>
> You can also roll the balls in coconut, crushed nuts, or raw carob or cacao powder.

PB&J Bites

These taste like my favorite Lara Bar, but without the added salt.

2 cups unsalted **PEANUTS**

1 cup pitted **DATES**

1 cup unsweetened **DRIED CHERRIES**

1 tablespoon alcohol-free **VANILLA**, or 1 teaspoon **VANILLA POWDER**

In a food processor fitted with the "S" blade, process the peanuts into a powder. Add the dates and cherries and process until a ball forms. Add the vanilla and process again briefly. Roll into balls or place in a silicone brownie mold pan.

> **CHEF'S NOTES:** For a lower-fat option, substitute 2 cups of rolled oats for the peanuts.

Peanut Butter Fudge Truffles

Two great tastes that taste great together

1 batch CHOCOLATE FUNDUE (page 136)

Chopped unsalted PEANUTS

Prepare the FUNdue, place in a glass bowl, and chill until firm. Use a small cookie scoop to form the FUNdue into balls and roll the balls in the chopped peanuts. Freeze until firm.

CHEF'S NOTES: I like to put these in individual paper candy cups. I'll also put these truffles inside See's Candies boxes and fool people all the time!

You can make a raw version of these treats by replacing the peanut butter in the FUNdue recipe with raw almond butter, raw cashew butter, or tahini and using chopped raw nuts instead of peanuts.

ACKNOWLEDGMENTS

Thank you to Dr. John McDougall and Mary McDougall for helping to launch my career in the plant-based movement by giving me my first big break in 2009 when I presented at their Celebrity Chef Weekend and my second and third big breaks when I presented at their 2011 and 2015 Advanced Study Weekends. More importantly, I thank them for their lifelong work, which is the basis of everything I teach and which has enabled thousands of people, including me, to regain our health and appearance and easily achieve our ideal weight, while stuffing our faces with potatoes.

Thank you to the enormously talented Hannah Kaminsky, whose photographs make my recipes look like works of art; to Rebecca Martinez, my wonderful sous-chef, for her invaluable recipe-testing; and to Doug Lisle, PhD, and Dr. Alan Goldhamer, DC, for teaching me how to get out of "the pleasure trap." I am forever grateful.

Thank you to Glen Merzer for making my words come to life on the page. And to you, dear reader, who is helping to save the planet by not eating animal products.

C hef AJ has followed a plant-exclusive diet for more than five decades. She was the host of the television series *Healthy Living with Chef AJ* which aired on FoodyTV She broadcasts *Chef AJ LIVE!* daily on YouTube. AJ lives with her handsome vegan husband Charles and their rescue mutt Bailey near Palm Springs, California. In 2018, she was inducted into the Vegan Hall of Fame and is proud to say that her IQ is higher than her cholesterol. She can be reached at ChefAJ.com.

G len Merzer has been vegetarian for almost fifty years and vegan for the last thirty. He is a playwright and screenwriter and the author or coauthor of eleven books advocating the vegan diet, including *Own Your Health* (featuring Chef AJ's recipes). His latest book, *Food Is Climate*, examines the climate emergency. He can be reached at glenmerzer.com.

Together, Chef AJ and Glen have collaborated on the original *Unprocessed*, the 10th anniversary edition of *Unprocessed, Own Your Health*, and the best-selling *The Secrets to Ultimate Weight-Loss*.

INDEX

Recipe names and photo references appear in italics.

books that educate, inspire, and empower

To find your favorite books on plant-based cooking and nutrition,
raw-foods cuisine, and healthy living, visit:

BookPubCo.com

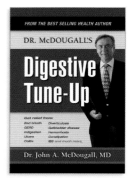

**Dr. McDougall's
Digestive Tune-Up**
John McDougall, MD
978-1-57067-184-5 • $19.95

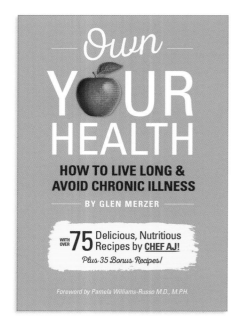

Own Your Health
How to Live Long & Avoid Chronic Illness
Glen Merzer with recipes by Chef AJ
978-1-57067-406-8 • $19.95

The Pleasure Trap
Mastering the Hidden Force
that Undermines Health & Happiness
Alan Goldhamer, DC, and Douglas J. Lisle, PhD
978-1-57067-197-5 • $16.95

Purchase these titles from your favorite book source or buy them directly from:
BPC • PO Box 99 • Summertown, TN 38483 • 1-888-260-8458

Free shipping and handling on all orders